KILLING TIME

WITH

JOHN WAYNE GACY

DEFENDING AMERICA'S MOST EVIL SERIAL KILLER ON DEATH ROW

KILLING TIME

WITH

JOHN WAYNE GACY

DEFENDING AMERICA'S MOST EVIL SERIAL KILLER ON DEATH ROW

KAREN CONTI

Black Lyon Publishing, LLC

KILLING TIME WITH JOHN WAYNE GACY
Defending America's Most Evil Serial Killer on Death Row

Copyright © 2024 by Karen Conti

All rights reserved.

No part of this book may be used or reproduced in any way
by any means without the written permission of the publisher,
except in the case of brief quotations embodied in critical articles
and reviews.

Please note that if you have purchased this book without a cover
or in any way marked as an advance reading copy, you have
purchased a stolen item, and neither the author nor the publisher
has been compensated for their work.

This is a work of non-fiction. All direct quotes are either from
recorded interviews, interviews with individuals by local
media at the time or the recollection of the individuals during
interviews with the author of what was said at the time. When
possible, those interviewed reviewed their recollected quotes for
accuracy.

Our books may be ordered through your local bookstore or by
visiting the publisher:

www.BlackLyonPublishing.com

Black Lyon Publishing, LLC
PO Box 567
Baker City, OR 97814

ISBN: 979-8-9865124-7-1
Library of Congress Control Number: 2023947897

Published and printed in the United States of America.

Black Lyon True Crime

PRAISE FOR THIS BOOK

"This **addictively readable** book about Karen Conti's representation of John Wayne Gacy, perhaps the most prolific serial killer ever to be put to death in this country, answers some of the law's most fascinating questions. Why would an outstanding attorney choose to represent a man who clearly contends for the title of 'worst of the worst?' And for those who oppose the death penalty, does that opposition remain even in a case like Gacy's, who tortured, murdered and disappeared 33 young men under the basement of his house?"
—Scott Turow, #1 *New York Times* bestselling author
Presumed Innocent* and *Ultimate Punishment

"*Killing Time* is **a testament to the human spirit's resilience**. Our protagonist, a woman navigating a male-dominated field, embodies the power of standing up for what's right, even when the world screams otherwise. Her journey is one of courage, empathy, and ultimately, self-discovery. Like many people who stand up for unpopular causes, Conti's experience strengthened her character and serves as an example for all."
—Sister Helen Prejean, author of the best-selling book,
Dead Man Walking, prominent anti-death penalty activist

"For those interested in the legal system: This book offers **a fascinating glimpse** into the challenges and ethical dilemmas faced by criminal defense attorneys!"
—Robert Shapiro, a member of the
"Dream Team" of O. J. Simpson's attorneys

"*Killing Time with John Wayne Gacy* is a **compassionate, articulate** narrative that demonstrates how it's possible to treat one of society's designated monsters as still human. As the only female attorney involved with Gacy's death penalty defense, Karen Conti offers an intimate sense of the serial killer as a person awaiting his execution. Her part in Gacy's story is **unique and engaging** while also making important points about American culture. This book should be required reading for anyone interested in criminal law or the criminal mind."
—Dr. Katherine Ramsland, professor of forensic psychology and award-winning author of ***Confession of a Serial Killer: The Untold Story of Dennis Rader, the BTK Killer***

MORE PRAISE FOR THIS BOOK

"... so well done and packed full of very credible information not only on Gacy but Conti's career and snippets of other cases. This book is **a must-read** for anyone who enjoys true crime with a twist. It's not just about the gruesome details; it's about the psychology of evil, the power of the legal system, and the unwavering strength of the human spirit."
—Ann Wolbert Burgess, Professor at Boston College, one of the original trailblazing "Mindhunter" FBI criminal profilers and author of *Killing by Design: Murders, Mindhunters, and My Quest to Decipher the Criminal Mind*

"I will never forget feeling the sheer confusion and horror described in this book, while I watched the news coverage: police carrying body bag after body bag out of the 'Gacy house' in a Chicago suburb. But in Karen Conti's disturbing memoir about her prison interviews with the notorious serial killer, she captures some things about his character that other Gacy books and made-for-TV movies have often flattened out: his weirdly commanding presence, and the insidious power in conversation that he must have turned upon his young victims. This is **not just 'another Gacy book.'** Ultimately, it becomes a **powerful** meditation on loss, grieving, and—surprisingly—the nature and limits of human compassion."
—Paul Edwards / Associate Professor Emeritus, Northwestern University, three-time Joseph Jefferson Award-winning playwright

"*Killing Time* quickly takes its place among the key writings on John Wayne Gacy. While providing new biographical information and insights, it explores the unique relationship a killer who exclusively targeted male victims developed with the only female attorney on either side of his case. It presents, moreover, **a wholistic picture** of someone commonly depicted as a one-dimensional colossus of evil, demonstrating that the most **frightening** quality of some serial predators is that, much of the time, they live and engage with others in a way that would prompt no bad feelings in the gut, nor cause any hairs on the backs of necks to stand up."
—Gary Brucato, Ph.D., Visiting Scholar at Boston College and co-author of *The New Evil: Understanding the Emergence of Modern Violent Crime.*

MORE PRAISE FOR THIS BOOK

"While many have exploited the story of John Wayne Gacy with varying degrees of success, *Killing Time with John Wayne Gacy* is a **completely refreshing** take. Karen Conti rolls out an **intimate tale** of her time representing one of the most famous serial killers during his last-ditch effort to overcome his death penalty sentence in 1994. Not only does she show herself as a professional and empathetic advocate for all manner of individuals ... she's one of the few women to engage with Gacy and lay bare his maze-like sociopathic mind. Conti picks up on small details other writers miss regarding the context of the culture, time, and location that are essential to understanding this case wasn't just about the worldwide sensation of a serial murderer. She acknowledges there was a political infrastructure around Gacy that enabled and protected him as he perpetrated unspeakable crimes. This is **a page-turner** that will further inform aficionados as well as those who are curious about what happens behind the closed doors of justice."
    —Tracy Ullman, Executive Producer of the Peacock Original docuseries ***John Wayne Gacy: Devil in Disguise***

"Karen Conti's book is **a fascinating look** at her time spent with the infamous serial killer John Wayne Gacy. Through Conti's story you may realize that your assumptions of a serial killer's personality may be far different than expected. Karen's story is gripping, and will have you hooked from page one. Do you think you have heard all there is to know about John Wayne Gacy? Well, you haven't until you have read Conti's book."
    —John Borowski, award-winning filmmaker/author, ***The John Wayne Gacy Murders: Life and Death in Chicago***

"*Killing Time* is not just an interesting look at 'America's Most Evil Serial Killer,' as told from the only woman lawyer representing John Wayne Gacy in the final flurry of legal appeals before his execution; it is also the story of how a sociopathic murderer changed the life and shaped the career of an idealistic young woman in the male-dominated legal profession. **Poignant, eye-opening, and humorous.**"
  —Andrea S. Kramer, Founder of ASKramer Law and author of ***Beyond Bias: The PATH to Ending Gender Inequality at Work***

Dedication

In memory of the life, love, and laughter of my father, Joe Conti.

———

I started writing this book 27 years after my representation of John Wayne Gacy ended. As a result, I have taken liberty with many of the conversations and descriptions and have expanded them consistent with my recollection. I have changed the names of clients and characters as nobody, even to this day, likes to be associated with John Gacy. As psychology professor Dr. Rosalind Cartwright said, "Memory is never a precise duplicate of the original ... it is a continuing act of creation." I hope that as the years have gone by and additional information has come to light, my memories have acquired the patina of wisdom, life experiences, and self-reflection.

—Karen Conti

1.

THE NIGHT BEFORE THE EXECUTION
May 9, 1994
10:45 p.m.

John Wayne Gacy, handcuffed and shackled, was escorted by five prison guards down the long hallway to his "waiting room" at the maximum-security Stateville Correctional Center, home to Illinois' death chamber. His last meal eaten (deep-fried shrimp, French fries, and Diet Coke), Gacy had said his goodbyes.

Members of his family who came to bid farewell had lingered, sobbing and praying together, unable to comprehend what was to happen. His neighbors were there, too—the neighbors who had lived next door to what became a private cemetery at 8213 W. Summerdale in Norwood Park, Illinois. Neighbors whose sidewalks Gacy plowed and whose appliances Gacy fixed. Little did they know while Gacy was plowing and fixing, he was also killing and burying corpses under his house, becoming a ghoulish funeral director of sorts.

I had said my goodbyes to my client hours earlier.

I was not permitted to be present at the execution, which was puzzling as the Constitution allows lawyers to be involved in every step of the criminal justice process. Once an arrested defendant requests a lawyer, one is permitted, and no further questioning can proceed without one. The lawyer is at trial and involved in every appellate brief and argument.

In the case of a capital defendant, there are many appeals. Gacy had over 20 of them. But in the end, when all legal actions are exhausted and all courts and judges have refused to change the verdict or the sentence and the governor refuses to issue a reprieve, the defendant is alone, facing death without any advocate beside him. I imagine taking the walk with him to his death.

The uniformed sheriff's officers huddle close to Gacy as they make their way to the waiting room, the place of detention until the last trip to the execution chamber. The guards are careful, not because they consider him an escape risk. Rather, they are making certain he cannot commit suicide before the needle can be inserted in his arm. How embarrassing it would be if Gacy cheated the State out of its right to execute him.

The officers lead him to a small room, its walls covered with peeling putty-colored paint. Several battered wooden chairs were pushed into the corner. Despite the depressing conditions, the condemned man, always a joker and a nonstop talker, chats with his keepers as if it were a country club outing.

"I wish you guys still used the electric chair. Ya know why?" Gacy asks, grinning.

One of the guards plays along. "Okay, John. Why?"

"Then my last request would be for you to hold my hand."

At some point, one of the more serious officers, not finding any of this banter funny, asks, "Seriously, Mr. Gacy, would you like to pray with me?"

Gacy declines, laughing, "Naw, God ain't taking calls today in honor of my execution. I already made my peace with God."

As always, Gacy has it under control ...

2.

THE CALL

Two days before I got the call that would change my life forever, I was driving through Chicago's west side with my law partner and life partner, Greg Adamski. It was October 1993, and I was a 29-year-old lawyer with six years under my Brooks Brothers belt, big shoulder pads and all. We were heading home to Oak Park, the first suburb west of the city.

The stressful workday was done and I was looking forward to putting on some comfortable clothes and having a glass of wine, not necessarily in that order. Driving west on Madison Street, we had just passed blocks of brownstones, once elegant, now boarded up and abandoned, pawn shops, liquor stores, empty lots, and old store-fronts-turned-churches, their names and congregation times painted by hand on white-washed boards. Despite the optimistic church names, the message was clear: Hope was a thing of the past.

Chicago has always been racially segregated and on the west side—which is mostly African-American—the neighborhood had long been starved of investment. Case in point: After crossing the border of Chicago and entering Oak Park, the homes immediately became larger, better kept, and markedly more expensive. Oak Park native Ernest Hemingway sarcastically described the village as a community of "broad lawns and narrow minds."

In 1993, it was just the opposite. The lawns were narrow

compared to the expansive lots in the newer suburbs, while the liberal-mindedness of Oak Parkers was legendary.

Dead leaves were in their fall finale, dropping wetly on the windshield and plastering the streets with their jagged shapes and colors, letting us know that another year was coming to a stark, cold end. Greg was at the wheel and I was in control of the radio. A voice came on telling us that we were listening to "WGN, the home of Chicago Cubs," a team which, as usual, had long been out of the running for post-season play.

As the drive-time news began, our ears perked up when we heard: "This morning, Governor Jim Edgar announced an execution date for serial killer John Wayne Gacy. Gacy, convicted of killing 33 boys and young men in suburban Norwood Park, is scheduled to die by lethal injection on May 10, 1994, at midnight at Stateville Correctional Center."

Greg turned to me. "They'll never execute Gacy. They haven't killed people in Illinois in ages."

He was right. I could not recall an Illinois execution.

In 1962, when I was just six months old, James Dukes was put to death in the electric chair in Cook County prison. Twenty-eight years went by with no executions. During that time, there was a brief countrywide moratorium on capital punishment after the U.S. Supreme Court ruled in *Furman v. Georgia* that the nation's death penalty laws as written constituted cruel and unusual punishment in violation of the 8th Amendment. Eventually, each state including Illinois rewrote its law, which cured the constitutional violation, and capital punishment was no longer deemed cruel and unusual. Four years before Gacy's death date was set, Illinois executed Charles Walker. There was no fanfare because he had waived his appeals, begging the state to take his life without further legal maneuvers. The death penalty had simply not been a prominent issue during my lifetime.

That said, I was never in favor of its use. My father reminded me of an incident that happened when I was seven years old—probably the first time I gave the issue any thought. While listening to our little transistor radio, there was talk about the use of capital punishment. My dad said to no one in particular, "Criminals who kill should be executed."

I turned to him and said, "Dad, wouldn't it still be a crime to kill someone even if they killed someone first?" I reasoned that the death penalty would be like being punished for not cleaning up my room by having someone mess up my room. No matter what we said to each other afterward, neither of us was persuaded to change our opinions.

I next encountered the issue in high school in a sociology class taught by a long-haired bearded young teacher named Jim Wilson who put us through hypothetical morality exercises. I remember taking the position that no matter what someone did, including killing everyone in the class, death should not be the punishment. Not a single classmate agreed with me, and I received a good amount of teenaged heat about it. That was my first experience with the fact that public opinion in this country is largely in favor of the death penalty.

Following those poignant memories, my attention turned back to Greg and our drive. I could hear the news had turned to sports and weather.

Greg repeated, "This execution is just not going to happen. Not even for Gacy."

For the next five minutes, we joked about how representing Gacy would be great for our business. Greg kidded, "After that, we could advertise ourselves as experts in "Clown Law." Not to be outdone, I devised a potential slogan: "Adamski & Conti: Come to our law firm with a traffic ticket. Leave with the death penalty."

I mused, "Wouldn't it be funny if we ended up representing him?" I meant funny as in bizarre, not humorous. Nothing about what this man did was laughable.

Greg and I continued our conversation, recalling Gacy's depraved crimes and where we were when the remains of over two dozen boys were removed from his home in suburban Norwood Park. I was a senior in high school on Christmas break. We talked about the 1979 trial. Gacy opted to lodge an insanity defense even though he was on record that he was against doing so. Greg and I both knew that insanity couldn't have worked because he knew his actions were wrong, a fact that defeats such a defense. If you bury so many boys under your home, it is probably because you are trying to hide your guilt, not because you like to dig! What other defense would we have lodged? Actual innocence? Fat chance. Gacy initially confessed, didn't he? How would we have attacked the search warrants? Was there probable cause to search? Would he now argue ineffective assistance of counsel to avoid the death penalty? Could Illinois' confusing jury instructions be an issue to overturn the death sentence? Would any appellate court be receptive to any argument? As they say: Bad facts make bad law. We were two lawyers Monday morning quarterbacking the handling of 14 years of legal wrangling. Tough case, we agreed. An understatement.

Greg and I had been practicing law in what we liked to call our boutique law firm. My translation of "boutique" is understaffed and underfunded. We were litigators, which means we handled cases that went to court as opposed to contract negotiation or drafting wills. The majority of our business was civil suits—the ultimate in legal oxymorons. There was nothing civil about people suing each other for money. We also handled criminal cases, but mostly for people accused of white-collar paper crimes with the occasional gun violation or burglary—all commonplace in Chicago. Neither of us had ever come close to confronting the reality of capital punishment; our conversations about it confined to dinner parties and intellectual debates among lawyers. Having a client facing execution wasn't in our wheelhouse.

Personally, my guilty pleasure throughout my life was reading up on serial killers, an interest that bordered on obsessive. My friends and I had an ongoing 15-year debate about the true identity of Jack the Ripper. I had once driven two hours out of my way on a road trip to visit Lizzie Borden's childhood home in Connecticut. *Buried Dreams*, the comprehensive book on John Gacy, was on my bedroom bookshelf along with *Stranger Beside Me*, the Ann Rule masterpiece about Ted Bundy. I had also followed with fascination the case of Jeffrey Dahmer, who had been tried one year before, just 90 miles north in Milwaukee. In short, I was a self-proclaimed serial killer junkie.

"Imagine knowing that you're going to die. John's gotta be shitting his pants about now," I said. As if the world's most prolific serial killer and I were on a first-name basis.

Little did I know: One week later we would be.

...

Two days after the execution was announced, we got "the call." I was toiling away on a long checklist of "to-dos" in my office on the 52nd floor at 70 West Madison, a bank building in the Chicago Loop. I was working on several domestic relations cases (nice way of saying divorces), an employment appeal for a plaintiff who was sexually harassed on the job, and a consumer fraud lawsuit. Greg normally called me into his office if he wanted to talk, but this time he charged into mine, eyes wide and face as red as a beet.

"You'll never guess who wants to see us!" Greg was almost hyperventilating. "Guess who wants us to represent him?"

"Give me a hint?"

"The most hated man in America," Greg said.

Without missing a beat, I ventured, "Richard Nixon?"

Greg blurted out, "Much worse! John Wayne Gacy."

"Oh my God. Holy shit!"

"Yeah, holy shit," Greg agreed.

Greg sat down and excitedly told me the whole story.

The call was from a lawyer representing Gacy's nephew.

Gacy wanted a "First Amendment lawyer" to represent him in a variety of civil matters, none of which, strangely, had anything to do with his rather serious impending criminal issues related to killing boys and then burying them under his home. Because Greg and I had recently handled a high-profile case on behalf of the Harold Washington Party (Chicago's third party at the time) before the U.S. Supreme Court on a First Amendment voters' rights issue, Gacy knew our names. Apparently, we were on the A list of free speech lawyers in Chicago, or at least from the viewpoint of this discriminating death row inmate. The fact that a serial murderer whose name was a household word knew ours was unsettling.

The Department of Corrections had sued him under an infrequently used statute that required incarcerated persons with assets to pay for the costs of their confinement. Gacy, protective of his pocketbook even in the face of impending lethal injection, wanted to fight the suit or as he publicly said, "If they want me to pay rent, they should just evict me."

The second issue involved the prison's attempts to enjoin him from selling his paintings—works of "art" that he produced prodigiously from Menard Correctional Center. Finally, the State wanted to shut down—get this for shameless enterprise—Gacy's 900 telephone hotline from which he professed his innocence and earned money to fund his prison lifestyle. Rightfully, government officials had received public criticism because their most notorious inmate was openly profiting from his crimes and notoriety. Death was not enough to punish Gacy; the prison officials wanted to take his money, too. And although he seemed incredibly arrogant defending his behavior, my curiosity pushed me to learn more.

After Greg told me every detail and nuance that I yanked out of him, he said to me, "This is all a bunch of bullshit. Why the hell does this guy want to fight this stuff when they're getting ready to off him?"

"Because he's crazy," I said, stating something of an obvious point, given Gacy's crimes.

Getting up, Greg looked over his shoulder, "I'll just call them back and tell them to forget about it."

I jumped out of my chair, banging my knees on my desk drawer. "Forget about it? We're going to pass up the chance to be in the presence of the world's most notorious serial killer? Come on. We have to at least meet him."

Greg's expression said, no we didn't.

"Okay. If you aren't going to go with me, I'll go alone."

I knew that would do it. Greg would never let me hang out on death row by myself. But still, he tried to reason with me. Why should we leave all of our paying business to drive six hours through the flat and tedious terrain of central Illinois to meet a man who was a known pathological liar and condemned to death? About what? These ridiculously frivolous legal issues we were being asked to handle on a pro bono basis? Why should we help a serial killer avoid a judgment against him when he is going to die in a few months? And why didn't he want us to address his death penalty case?

But at that moment, I was oblivious to reality. "Greg, imagine the stories we'll be able to tell at cocktail parties about how we met the world's most prolific serial killer. Don't you want to know what it's like to stare evil in the eyes?"

After a wry reference to the evil of his ex-wife, Greg began to see the allure of a road trip culminating in the legal adventure of a lifetime, meeting the guiltiest, least remorseful, and most despised man in the world.

Gacy's arrogance and lack of respect for all things decent were well known and, as I have often said, at least Jeffrey Dahmer had the grace to be pathetic.

It was agreed. We would road-trip downstate to Menard Correctional Center in rural Chester, Illinois to meet the poster child for the death penalty. The best part was that we had not committed to do anything for him except meet him.

However, I would soon learn that curiosity, besides killing cats, can change the direction of your life forever.

3.

FLASHBACK

As I contemplated the road trip to death row, my thoughts flashed back to where and who I was when the Gacy crimes were literally unearthed. In 1978, I was a 16-year-old senior at Morton West High School in Berwyn, a suburb just west of Chicago. Jokingly referred to by my father as the home of the "Tomb of the Unknown Bowler," Berwyn housed 60,000 blue-collar workers and all the Pabst Blue Ribbon that came with them.

Many residents at that time had moved out of Chicago in "white flight" and landed in the bungalows that lined the neat grid of streets. Although the town is more diverse now, back then it was very white and not welcoming of people of color.

In the summer of 1979, when Gacy was preparing for trial, the Nazis came to Illinois and marched in two places: Skokie, and Berwyn; Skokie because they hoped to offend the largely Jewish community, and Berwyn because they thought they had a fan base there. Despite being raised in a town known for its closed-mindedness, I was taught to think otherwise. My parents did not tolerate racial or ethnic slurs and would not hesitate to punish such language with a slap to my face.

My home was politically Democratic but ruled by a notably undemocratic mother. Marilyn was from a German family in rural Kentucky. She had her good points: Early to bed and early to rise. Do your homework. Eat your vegetables. As

I look back now, I believe my mother may have had borderline personality disorder, which caused her to launch into frequent and sudden rages and traumatized all of us—and then ceased with no apparent adverse effect on her.

My father was the opposite. The first son of Italian immigrants, he was all affection, fun, and spontaneity. Born into a coal mining family in southern Illinois, Joe's parents honored the Italian tradition of binding his feet together at birth to keep evil spirits out of his soul. The feet binding thing backfired because at age of ten, Joe became a world-class tap dancer, later winning the national Major Bowes competition, that era's radio version of *American Idol*. (My father shared his award with a then-unknown singer named Frank Sinatra and his group, "The Hoboken Four.")

After moving to Hollywood and appearing in several movies as one of the Dead End Kids, my father became a stand-up comedian for four decades entertaining audiences in nightclubs like the Playboy Club, comedy clubs, and private venues. While I love touting his accomplishments, the downside was the unpredictable paychecks he earned while my unpredictable mother stayed at home to raise us.

Growing up in a household polarized by the creative and freeform work habits of my father and the carefully structured parameters and expectations of my mother, I navigated a tightrope. I was a typical middle child, finding it unfair not to have the preferential freedom of movement my older brother enjoyed or the privilege of being coddled like my younger sister. Those inequities, my desire to help the underdog, and a yearning for a financially stable life surely led to the career I chose.

When Gacy's name was about to become a household word, one synonymous with evil, I was at the top of my game. I was an honor student, vice president of the class, and on three sports teams. I took piano lessons and was the first chair flute in the band. I was voted Most Likely to Succeed. I had taken up "jogging" (still in fad status) and was listening to the music of the Little River Band. Unlike many of my cohorts, I charted an ambitious future that included college and then law school.

I dreamed of taking the train every morning to my storefront office in downtown Chicago wearing beautiful wool suits and high-heeled pumps. Not knowing a single lawyer up to that point in my life, I thought I would represent criminal clients, but I never imagined that any one of them might be guilty.

While enjoying my 1978 Christmas break, luxuriating in watching the morning game shows like *Let's Make a Deal*, *The Price Is Right*, and *Hollywood Squares* playing back-to-back on the three networks, a news story aired that shocked me to the core. It is a story that caught my attention as a kid and would pull me in again 14 years later as a lawyer.

The hunt for a missing 15-year-old boy, Rob Piest, brought police to the doorstep of a very neat, suburban home owned by a successful construction contractor and remodeler, John Wayne Gacy.

After getting a warrant for his house, police uncovered one set of remains that was *not* Rob Piest. The discovery was terrifying but we had no idea what was to come.

A day later, the news showed another stretcher being carried out of the house—and then another.

Hour after hour, stretchers topped with black body bags emerged from this house of horror, carrying out the excavated remains. The number of victims was staggering. Just when you thought five was it, there were two more. Three more. I heard my bus driver neighbor talking to my dad on our front porch about how co-workers at the Chicago Transit Authority had placed bets on how many bodies there would eventually be. My dad, who was a lover of betting on anything, exercised great restraint from throwing his money in the pot. My neighbor likely lost money because he had wagered on the number seven.

Eventually, we learned that there were the tragic remains of 26 young men—sons, brothers, some husbands and fathers—in the crawlspace. I didn't know what a crawlspace was and had to ask my mother. Three other bodies were buried on Gacy's property, and four additional bodies were found later in the Des Plaines River for a total of 33 victims. According to reporters, these men and boys had likely been sexually molested and Gacy was the lone wolf responsible.

Like a lot of teens from the era, I didn't understand rape and sexual torture. Every year, we all saw the film *Stranger Danger* and were taught not to talk to people we didn't know, take candy from them, or get into their cars. We thought that was because those bad men would simply steal us and never let us see our parents again. In my suburban 1970s world, I could not comprehend what someone like John Gacy was all about.

The victims were described as "homosexuals," "hustlers," and "drug users," all of which held horrendous connotations for the morality of the time. Homosexuality had been taken off the list of official mental disorders by the DSM just a few years before. Closeted homosexuals were the norm, many hiding in legitimate marriages to avoid the stigma. As I sit here now, I don't remember having an understanding of homosexuality. There were boys in school who others teased and called "queer" and "homo," but I didn't understand what any of that meant. Although his victims' faces made it on screen, it was hard to relate to young men who, by the way the media portrayed them, could almost be deemed responsible for their own deaths because of their lifestyle choices.

Three days after my 18th birthday, Gacy was tried in Chicago before a jury bussed in from nearby Rockford, the trial judge deciding that Chicago jurors would be too prejudiced by the incredible pretrial publicity. For nine summers while he was preparing for trial, being convicted, and filing appeals, I worked as a lifeguard at the local municipal swimming pool. Ironically, during those years I held a Red Cross certification as a "Lifesaver."

I could never imagine that when my days of sunny summer jobs ended, I would be tasked with attempting to save the life of a man who had already drowned well before I got to him.

4.

THE ROAD TO PERDITION

On the Monday following "the call," Greg and I set out on our road trip to Menard Correctional Center in downstate Chester, Illinois.

Gacy and his Chicago "handlers" who introduced us made it clear he wanted a "whole day" with his visitors. We were to arrive as early as possible and stay as long as possible. Although it made no sense that a condemned killer could be demanding given his circumstances, and despite our not being paid for our time, we were compliant. We learned early on that there is a thin line between fame and infamy, repulsion and fascination. Gacy perversely garnered respect due to his record-setting crimes and name recognition. We later learned that Gacy had a way of getting what he wanted within the prison walls—privileges others were not given with money from his 900 number and paintings greasing the wheels. As bad as he was, he was good at his badness and used that status with others around him to manipulate them. We were not in a position to argue.

We awoke reluctantly to the strident alarm clock buzz at 2:30 a.m. startling my cat, Madison, who had the feline sense to know that it was not yet feeding time. Without showers or too much thought, we dressed quickly in business attire and were out the door of our Oak Park home as scheduled at 3 a.m. My briefcase contained a dog-eared copy of *Buried Dreams*, the Tim Cahill book about Gacy and his crimes, and a manilla folder stuffed with appeal briefs and court decisions from the past 14 years, which I had asked my law clerk to print out the Friday before.

I had also packed my makeup bag so at some point during the trek, when there was light, I could make myself presentable to the most prolific serial killer in the world. For me, vanity was a habit, not a choice. With a thermos of strong black coffee and a small cooler of fruit, bagels, and orange juice stowed in the back seat of our sturdy Mercedes sedan, we set off on our prison-bound excursion.

It was a typical late October morning in the Midwest, although I had not seen such an early October morning since my college days of all-nighters. The streets were empty, and it was pitch black, the sun yet to consider making its way toward the horizon. The majority of the leaves had fallen, and the suburban streets were matted with a slick mess of gold and brown. Greg drove and I was the designated navigatrix. The directions, however, were not that complicated: Head south and keep going until you hit the Mississippi River. There was no GPS back then and none was needed.

Illinois is a long state—one that holds clashing cultural and social mores as you travel from north to south. Chicagoland is a bustling, liberal, fast-paced urban mecca where we worked and played. Moving toward the south of the state, there is a slower pace, southern charm, rural camaraderie, and a love of guns and traditional values. My theory is that there are two parts to the United States: One that serves grits and the other that doesn't know what they are. That morning drive took us through both parts of the country.

In 20 minutes, we were motoring south on Interstate 57, which would take us almost all the way to Chester. Sipping coffee and munching on breakfast, I used a penlight to peruse *Buried Dreams* to bone up on my Gacy facts. I skimmed the pages, reading portions aloud that described his childhood, family relationships, young adulthood, and initiation into the life of murder—the details of his rise to the bottom.

Gacy was born on March 17, 1942, in Chicago, the second

child and only son of middle-class parents. His father was an auto-repair machinist who named his son after John Wayne, the Hollywood western actor considered the epitome of masculinity. His mother was a homemaker. He was close to his mother and two sisters, but had a difficult relationship with his father, an alcoholic who physically and verbally abused his wife and children. His father made a habit of belittling him, calling him "dumb and stupid." His mother's efforts to protect him from his father's abuse backfired, resulting in the elder Gacy calling his son a "sissy" and a "Mama's boy"—and telling him he would "probably grow up queer."

Greg and I discussed this upbringing and debated whether Gacy's dysfunctional background was enough to turn him to a life of murder. Greg, who was just a few years younger, contended that Gacy's family dynamic was not dissimilar from the upbringing of many of his friends and the way children were raised at that time in that culture. Ultimately, we came to the conclusion if those friends didn't become murderers, Gacy's environment could only have played a minor role in his predilections.

I skipped to the part of the book that described Gacy's young adulthood. After a stint as a mortuary worker in Las Vegas where it was believed he slept in a coffin with one of the corpses, Gacy returned to Illinois and became a management trainee at a shoe company in Springfield, Illinois' state capitol. There, he met and married a co-worker, Marlynn Myers. The couple moved to Waterloo, Iowa where Marlynn's father had purchased three Kentucky Fried Chicken restaurants at which Gacy was the manager.

Initially, Gacy was seen as upholding his father-in-law's entrepreneurial legacy and the two settled into a home Marlynn's father purchased for them and their two children. Gacy earned a salary that was the equivalent of $115,000 in today's dollars plus a share of the restaurants' profits. Life seemed to be going well for the young man and finally, his father was proud of him.

Gacy's seemingly charmed life fell apart in 1967 when he was charged with sexual assault of one of his 15-year-old employees and an attempted sexual assault of another teenager, who was the son of a state senator. After charges were brought, he then paid an 18-year-old employee to physically assault one of the victims in an attempt to dissuade him from testifying. This brought additional charges for assault and intimidation.

The court ordered Gacy to undergo a psychiatric evaluation. After 17 days, two doctors diagnosed him with antisocial personality disorder and concluded he was unlikely to benefit from any therapy or medical treatment. They also predicted that his behavior pattern was likely to bring him into "repeated conflict with society." Had they only known ...

Despite this, Gacy was deemed to be mentally competent to stand trial. After pleading guilty to one count of assault, he went to trial on the other counts. He was found guilty and sentenced to ten years in an Iowa prison. His wife filed for divorce and obtained custody of their two children, changing their names and attempting to live in anonymity.

Many believe that what happened in Waterloo, Iowa was indicative of behaviors he potentially learned in Chicago and then Springfield while he was developing a relationship with members of the Democratic political establishment.

In his Waterloo court case, there are interviews with individuals who talk about Gacy, as president of the Jaycees social organization, attempting to entice new members using booze and stag films—not really part of the Jaycees "brand" that touted "leadership training and civic organization."

Another court transcript has a teenage boy describing being secured to a bed and forced by Gacy to have sex with Marlynn. Even Gacy's younger sister, Karen, talks about arriving in Waterloo and facing the expectation that she and her husband would go "swinging" with Marlynn and John. All of these are indications that Gacy was shameless about his illicit sexual behaviors.

Even in light of the deviant nature of his crimes and potential recidivism, Gacy was paroled after serving only 18 months of his ten-year sentence. A Chicago restaurateur, Eugene Boschelli, vouched that he would give Gacy a job and Gacy's mother agreed that he could live with her—two conditions that are often required to successfully receive parole.

Greg and I speculated: At this point, could he have been rehabilitated? He was brought up Catholic and was homosexual or at least bisexual. This presented a huge conflict in his life, but did it cause him to rape victims rather than simply engage in consensual relationships?

Did the shortened incarceration embolden Gacy to hit the ground running in Chicago to embark on his frenzy of rapes and murders? After Iowa, did he understand that going forward, he had to kill his victims so as not to leave any witnesses? Or did his obsessive urgings simply escalate, requiring more intense violence to satisfy his cravings? With corn fields and sleepy little towns continuing to whiz by in the background, we speculated about human conduct: At what point is a person so damaged and so decidedly evil that there is a point of no return?

Central Illinois is flat, so flat they say that you can watch your dog run away for three weeks. We were about two and a half hours into our trip when I spotted the sign for "Champaign," home to University of Illinois, the 44,000-student-populated state institution where I attended law school. A shiver of difficult memories and nostalgia ran through my body. Working my way through school with odd jobs and scholarships, I spent three grueling and stressful years attaining my lifetime goal of being a lawyer. While some students enjoy law school, I sure didn't. My favorite part of law school was taking that final drive north on I-57 after graduation.

However, those difficult years had served me well, taking me from an unemployable political science major and turning me into a lawyer with a pedigree from what was at the time one of the top 20 law schools in the nation. I laughed to myself. Could I have ever imagined as I sat in my criminal law class that I would someday be asked to use my degree to defend a serial killer?

It was still dark and the highway nearly desolate except for long-haul truckers speeding by trying to make their deliveries on schedule. We passed a number of small towns: Tuscola, Mattoon, Effingham, Arcola, and Mount Vernon. Many of

Illinois' most populated prisons were along this route: Pinckneyville, Centralia, Ina (Big Muddy), Vandalia and the federal prison in Marion where New York mobster, John Gotti, spent his last days of incarceration. Many of these "prison towns" survive only because of the existence of these institutions. The business of keeping criminals behind bars employs lots of people to support the motels and fast-food restaurants frequented by those making the long trip downstate to visit their incarcerated loved ones.

As the sun began peeking over the horizon, we turned off I-57 and followed the winding route of smaller roads leading to our destination. These narrow rural lanes gave us a closer look at some of the small towns along the way: Dix, which evoked a childishly rude joke from Greg, Steelville and then Bremen, named after the home village of the Grimm Brothers, author of popular, but dark children's books. Twisting and turning, we wound our way to the town of Chester, one hour south of St. Louis and on the same latitude as Louisville, Kentucky.

Pulling into town, I glanced at my watch. 8:40 a.m. We made good time. Following the signs along the way to the prison, we noted one warning a "Do Not Pick Up Hitchhikers"—never a good idea anywhere, but probably a really bad idea where there were 2,000 convicted murderers living close by—men who would love nothing more than a free ride out of town.

Weary from the long drive with stiff legs, Greg and I pulled up to Menard Correctional Center. At the entrance to the visitor's area, we paused, taking in the grandness of the building. Lurking on the banks of the Mississippi River with the sun glinting off its stone façade was a Gothic monstrosity, home to some of the most dangerous criminals in Illinois history.

Wired on coffee and carbs, we had spent our six hours productively and knew what we needed to know about Illinois' most famous inmate, John Wayne Gacy. He killed 33 boys and men and buried most of them under his house. He lost his trial and for the past 14 years, lost every single issue in every appeal filed on his behalf and, if the death penalty was going to be used, he was a dead man.

5.

THE NIGHT BEFORE THE EXECUTION
May 9, 1994
11:04 p.m.

The guards stand in the small waiting room with Gacy, shifting from foot to foot, whispering among themselves. The atmosphere is thick with tension. This is not a normal part of their jobs and they are not comfortable with this task. The Department of Corrections had chosen the biggest and most senior staff to accompany Gacy during his final moments but gave them the option not to participate if they were opposed. Some wanted the assignment, knowing this was a historic event they could talk about long after their careers were over.

Gacy was not expected to resist. He was never a tough guy, nor was he athletic or coordinated. His father and schoolmates made fun of him throughout his childhood for being a wimp. He sure showed them. He sure became a tough guy when he slapped handcuffs on his victims, doused them with chloroform, held their heads underwater, and sodomized them while he ended their lives with pain and terror being their last experiences on Earth. This time, the cuffs were on him, and the chemicals that would soon course through his veins were much stronger than anything in his arsenal of torture devices.

Several minutes go by. Then suddenly, all conversation stops and the room goes silent. From the hallway comes the echo of footsteps and the jangling of keys. The heavy pockmarked door opens. It is the prison warden come to pay his respects.

The civility of it all.

Gacy straightens himself, tilts his chin up slightly, immersed in his own importance. Tonight, he is the VIP (Very Important Prisoner).

In one hour, he will once again make history by being the most prolific murderer in history to be executed. He stands, all 5'9" inches of him. His paunchy body and pasty white skin remind anyone who sees him where he has been for the past 14 years: in a cage with the other people whom society has decided must pay for the deaths they caused with the currency of their own lives.

The prison warden addresses Gacy like a business associate, shakes his hand firmly. "How ya doin', John? Feeling okay today?"

"Sure thing, Mr. Warden." He appears respectful, unflappable, and rule-abiding. No indication of the man who conducted his life as if the basic laws of humanity did not apply to him.

The warden takes out two cigars from his suit coat pocket and hands one to Gacy. "Care for a last smoke, John?"

"Shit no. That stuff'll kill you."

He takes the cigar anyway, and the warden lights them both.

After a few puffs, the warden looks at Gacy, all kidding aside. There is a purpose for his visit.

"Now I want to tell you what is going to happen, John. So there are no surprises. We're gonna take you from here, walk you down the hall to the chamber. We'll strap you on the gurney. You can say your final words if you want. The witnesses will be in the room in front of you. About 25 of 'em ... You probably won't see them 'cause there's gonna be lights shining in your face. You'll get the first shot and you should be asleep in seconds."

"Got it, Mr. Warden. Let's get this done. You probably got better things to do today."

With that, the head honcho of this hell-hole shakes hands with Gacy, God-blesses him and nods to the guards who are huddled in the corner.

6.
LIFE AWAITING DEATH

Exiting our car in the visitors' lot, we looked up at the looming edifice before us. Menard Correctional Center: There is nothing that will be corrected here, I thought. Known unfondly as "The Pit," the prison was built in 1878—13 years after the Civil War ended—and was designed to house 1,600 inmates. With double that population, Menard was the largest maximum-security prison in the state and was also the most dangerous one. Judges had repeatedly found the conditions "inhumane" and cells "shockingly small." Assaults on both guards and other inmates were common and, through the years, numerous guards and prisoners had lost their lives. This was hardly surprising because two out of three men housed here were convicted murderers.

The facility's amber limestone, sourced from the 30-foot bluffs that towered over the prison, melded into the riot of colorful foliage swaying over the Mississippi River. Razor wire topped the tall walls and the manned guard tower reminded us that this was not a historic tour. The prison's imposing façade boasted ornate carvings and insignias, which probably had some meaning when it was designed but were lost on the guards who were required to pay attention to avoiding inmate attacks rather than appreciating the architectural significance of their workplace.

I wondered if any of the men behind these walls would be able to describe the building's exterior since their passage through the Pit's portico was generally a one-way street.

There was an atmosphere of despair and decay surrounding what could have been an insane asylum from a Stephen King-inspired movie set.

Opening the car doors, I could smell the earthy scent of Old Man River, the mighty Mississippi. How many stories of glory, prosperity, and death had this river seen? What tortured souls had spent huge portions of their lives behind these stone walls? As we walked toward the entrance of the facility, I realized it was at least 15 degrees warmer than when we departed. It felt like the South.

The sun danced in and out from behind wispy clouds, and a ghostly mist hid part of the prison. I could hear our car's cooling engine ticking like a metronome, a dark reminder of the limited time the subject of this trip had left to live. At the entrance, we paused once again. Looking into each other's eyes, Greg and I silently agreed that we would make the most of this trip. Meeting a killing machine who is condemned to death is an experience that most human beings never have. There was really nothing to lose as most of what had happened to this man had already been lost.

Wired on coffee and carbs, walking toward the entrance, we passed two stone lions sitting at ease atop brick bases. Their position of repose told us that their courage and strength would not be necessary to keep order here as 180 armed guards were doing that job. We proceeded under an awning to the door of the intake area, passing several uniformed employees who were smoking and drinking cans of Pepsi. They eyed us warily. Our business attire identified us as lawyers and big-city ones at that. We said our good mornings which were acknowledged by wary glances and subtle disapproving head nods.

Prisons, by definition, are unsafe places. However, I believed that when it came to lawyers, there was honor among inmates because we were generally there to help get someone out. If one person succeeded in beating the system, perhaps others would follow suit. People have repeatedly asked me if I was afraid of visiting Gacy. The answer is no—not the first time or any time. As a potential victim, I was not his type. I also knew his particular sociopathic tendencies were controlled enough not to harm a person he could use and manipulate. That said, I did not share the same confidence in the ability of other characters on death row to control their conduct. Many of them suffered from untreated mental health issues and had nothing to lose—a bad combination.

One thing I learned by visiting prisons is that you must respect the guards. They are the only ones keeping you safe from inmates. Corrections officers also have options as to when and how they intervene once an inmate problem arises, and you don't want them to hesitate to step in because you have treated them disrespectfully.

Inside the visitors' area, we crossed a tiled floor and headed toward the intake desk. Prisons embrace protocol, so you must make your arrangements carefully before you take a long drive to see an inmate. I had once driven four hours to a facility, only to be happily turned away by an officious and self-important guard who insisted that my registration was not on record, even though I had written confirmation of it in my hand.

We stepped up to the desk to face a seated intake guard. After a good 90 seconds of flipping through the large visitor sign-in book for no apparent reason, he looked up as if he did not know we were there waiting.

"Now, how can I help you today?" he drawled, his accent sounding like one from Alabama, not Illinois.

"We're here to see John Gacy," Greg said.

With a smirk, the guard said, "Good old JW. Let me see if he's in today." Prison humor at its best.

"Need your state IDs, attorney IDs. All personal property out of your pockets. Lockers are on your right. They take quarters. Nothing goes in except eyeglasses and coins for vending. Metal detector and a manual search in the next room."

Rules for visits were different for attorneys. We were not required to be on the visitor list, but we did need to pre-register our attorney visit, which we had done. Correctional facilities are compelled to treat lawyers preferentially due to right-to-counsel issues and years of lawsuits brought by inmates alleging they were denied the ability to consult with their attorneys while behind bars. That did not mean lawyers were treated any better by the guards.

We emptied our pockets, removed our jewelry, and placed it in the ancient, rusted lockers lining the wall. We kept a handful of quarters from our change jar at home. Prisoners look forward to vending machine food which they can usually get only when visitors buy it for them, so we always made sure we had quarters for these kinds of visits. It is such a pathetic thing to see an inmate get excited about a Milky Way, but when you have been denied decent food for years, you might feel the same way. We take so many freedoms for granted and visiting a prison magnifies that fact.

With belongings secured, a uniformed male guard ushered us into the next room. Passing through the metal detector, I noted the thick, drab concrete walls around us with signs warning about the ramifications of bringing in contraband such as drugs, hacksaws, hypodermic syringes, and explosive devices.

Once through the detector, Greg and I were separated. I was brought to a small room where I waited ten minutes for a female guard to search me. It's hard to take it personally when you are searched, but this one seemed unduly severe and degrading with the guard touching every part of my breasts, crotch, and toes with the finesse of a teenage boy.

Outside the search room, Greg and I were reunited. His facial expression told me his search was just as invasive as mine.

One officer led us one officer through a hallway to a large heavy door. He unlocked it and admitted us into a small antechamber. He slammed the door shut and relocked it, leaving us in there for five long minutes while he walked around to the other side to open the door leading out of the area. The purpose was obviously to prevent a visitor from wresting away the key ring from the jailer while in the enclosed area together. The effect of being confined for those few moments was a taste of what the residents here endured for years on end.

We continued to walk through maze-like hallways, and the lock-in process was repeated several times. As we made our way deeper and deeper into the 46-acre prison facility, the smells assaulted me: A combination of stale sweat and mildew, smells of a facility that had housed horrendous evils, yet standing solid in its filth and despair.

At some point, another guard joined us, and we were led through a courtyard where the grass was neatly manicured and the leaves raked. I wondered if inmates were used for labor as they are in many correctional facilities. Suddenly, the cheers and shouts began. I saw the faces of hundreds of prisoners looking and gesturing through bars, most of them with black and brown skin and most of them in some state of undress. Thankfully, the cacophony of whistles, hoots, and hollers drowned out any one voice and I did not hear anything too offensive, not that this was a time to be overly sensitive. Seeing a woman who wasn't dressed in a guard's uniform was apparently a reason for revelry.

I felt a veil of sadness come over me as I always do when I am in a prison. What horrific acts did these men commit to cause their lives to devolve into this depressing existence? Was it a spur-of-the-moment lapse in judgment or a lifetime of violent acts? Did they spend their days reflecting on the errors they made, or do they consider themselves victims of society? Will any of them ever leave this building on their own two feet or will they be carried out in a body bag?

At the end of the yard, we entered a building that was identical to the others. I realized that we had arrived at Death Row.

Entering a small room set up as an office, several officers were seated behind desks looking out over the visitors' area. They had the empty stare of bouncers surveying a nightmarish nightclub. I don't frighten easily, but these men were scary. My impression was they enjoyed exerting force and would gladly exercise their power over anyone they could. Their expressions were of amusement, particularly directed at me. Who is this woman and why is she visiting John Gacy? I immediately understood that he had probably never had a female attorney visitor; all of his attorneys over 14 years had been male.

The guards' attention was largely focused on scanning the visitors' area. I expected, when visiting a death row inmate, Greg and I would be in an enclosed stall sitting across from an inmate behind thick Plexiglas just like in the movies. As I peered through the smeared glass into the visiting area, I saw this was not at all the case. The visiting room consisted of several small-windowed, doorless cubicles on either side of a central walkway. Prisoners were seated next to or across a table from their visitors with no barriers between or among inmates or visitors. Inmates roamed free-range, chatting with others.

I spotted our guy in the third cubicle on the right. When he saw us through the window, he stood up eagerly, clearly anxious for us to join him. One of the guards unlocked the door with a loud buzzer and manually opened the heavy door for us with a wave of his hand to where Gacy was standing.

"Thank you," I whispered, and we stepped across the airless threshold. The door slammed behind us with a clank and a buzz. Like most lawyers who do criminal work, I was familiar with who was on death row, and I immediately recognized several high-profile inmates. I quickly calculated that the number of victims murdered at the hands of the men in this room would field at least five baseball teams, Gacy alone being responsible for more than three of them.

As we approached Gacy, I looked around, noting the cinder block walls were painted a sickly beige. Each cubicle had either an old metal desk or a wood laminate round table with metal folding chairs on either side. The inmates were dressed in prison blue and were hosting a varied crew of visitors, including what appeared to be lawyers, ministers, and family members. It struck me that we were locked in a bullpen with the worst criminals in the state with no way to alert the authorities if someone were to attack us. I firmly believed the guards would be of no use even if they did care enough to come to the rescue. They just wouldn't be able to act quickly enough. While I trusted the world's most prolific serial killer not to attack me ... the others, not so much.

Meeting Gacy was all about throwing preconceived notions out the window. While I knew he was not going to appear as a ghoulish evil character from a horror movie, with blood dripping from his sharpened fangs, I was not prepared for how small and unimposing he was, especially considering the number and brutality of crimes he had committed. The first thing I noticed about him was an aura of unhealthiness. Fourteen years of incarceration is not a trip to the spa; it is a combination of bad food, lack of exercise, no sunshine, incredible stress, and the absence of adequate dental work and hygiene. Death row inmates are typically not allowed to go outside very often and many of them choose not to do so for security reasons. They learn to dwell within the walls of their tiny cells.

Gacy was 5'9"—a far cry from the 6' 2" of Brian Dennehy, who portrayed him in the made-for-television movie, *Killer Clown*. He was overweight with the majority of his excess pounds protruding over his waistband. The word "dumpy" came to mind. His face was ashen, splotchy, and bloated. A dimpled chin and several beneath it were wedged against his blue prison-issue shirt. His hair was greasy—and you could see the comb marks from the front of his head to the back; this was due either to lack of washing or the use of some sort of hair pomade. I had seen this face so many times in documentaries, magazines, and news reports that it was surreal to see him in the flesh. There was nothing attractive about Gacy and his light blue eyes were somehow flat and lacking in depth or warmth. They exuded distrust and evasiveness.

Upon closer inspection, Gacy had tried to look his best. His prison shirt and pants were without wrinkles and tucked in appropriately. He was clean-shaven and smelled of a sweet drugstore cologne. Prisoners do not get to shower very often—in Gacy's case, once a week—so aftershave, purchased in the commissary, was often used to mask the smell of sweat and unwashed skin.

The last things I noticed were his hands. They were smooth and well-manicured, almost dainty. They were in stark contrast to the gunmetal gray of the thick handcuffs binding them together. A thought flashed through my head that he was in the same shackled position as many of his victims when they were brutally raped, tortured, and murdered. He held out his hands to shake ours and in his best nasal Chicago accent (think Saturday Night Live's skit "Da Bears") said plainly, "I'm John Gacy. How're you doin'?"

There is nothing from your upbringing, education, or life experiences that prepares you for having a conversation with a serial killer. What to say and what not to say? You cannot act horrified that you are talking to someone who you know is guilty of heinous acts, but at the same time, you cannot get them out of your mind. Interacting with Gacy that day and throughout was very confusing. The simple human exchanges felt strange knowing that, despite his outward normalcy, this man was simply not wired like any other human being I had ever met. And while I had experience dealing with many a narcissist and sociopath in my personal and legal life, this level of disordered personality was in a category of its own. If John Gacy didn't think like a normal person but acted like one, which one of those people was I dealing with?

We sat down at the table across from Gacy. I find that men who meet for the first time start comparing notes about safe topics like sports and driving directions. Gacy and Greg were no different. Gacy politely asked us about our trip—what route we took, where we stopped along the way, how long it took, how was the traffic, were the leaves colorful? He chatted about the perennial losing Chicago Cubs and Greg, an inveterate baseball fan, was happy to commiserate with Gacy about their fourth-place finish that season. "Anyone can have a bad century," he quipped, quoting one of Chicago's long-time Cubs announcers.

Right from the start, I noted Gacy was unusually talkative, glib. It was as if he did not want there to be a moment of empty silence between us. I would later learn that serial killers usually have good verbal skills and a high degree of intelligence, enough to lure victims into vulnerable positions. He moved quickly from topic to topic. He gave the impression of being intelligent, but uneducated, smattering his sentences with ain'ts and other grammatical errors. He spoke out of the corner of his mouth, giving him a smirking expression. His demeanor exuded haughtiness like he was smarter than anyone in the room, a know-it-all. But there was a charm there, too; charm that had served him well both in his quest to lure victims and to later cover his culpability.

We spoke about life in prison, which was always interesting to an outsider. How was the food? (Terrible. The commissary had better food.) How often did they get out? (Once a week, but he generally did not opt to go outside.) Did he read newspapers? (Yes, but a week after they came out.) How many visitors were he allowed per month? (Five, but with his death date set, they were a little more lenient.)

At this point, Greg asked if Gacy had a television. He told us that almost all inmates had a television. We knew from visiting other prisoners that guards and the jail administration are in favor of anything and everything that keeps inmates busy and happy and not attacking them and each other. Television was the prime prison pacifier. Gacy told us that Menard had a closed-circuit channel that allowed inmates to watch movies. He explained that several "lifers" were in charge of using the prison's small budget to purchase, among other things, second-run movies for the channel. This same group organized family picnics on the grounds and various sporting activities. While the "deathers" were not allowed to go outside for the picnics and softball games, they were allowed to watch movies.

Greg then asked a question that I thought violated all codes of how to deal with a serial killer. "Hey John, have you seen *Silence of Lambs*?"

Gacy nodded. "Sure have. Great movie."

"Did it scare you?" For that, Greg received an under-the-table kick from me.

With his vacant blue eyes, Gacy first looked at Greg and then turned to me with a frown of mock puzzlement. He put his head down and shook it in the negative. "Naw. I wasn't scared. You hafta understand, youse guys. When someone like me watches a movie like that ... I'm rooting for the killer."

"Oh," Greg and I responded in unison.

At this point, Gacy put his head back and laughed. Serial killer joke number one.

We continued our small talk and five minutes later, Gacy bluntly broached the topic of vending machine food. It was clear he was really looking forward to this.

I stood up offering to do the honors. "What would you like, John? I'm buying."

"Pretzels, M&Ms, and a Diet Coke." He had clearly thought it out.

"Will do. Greg, vodka martini?"

"That would hit the spot." Greg's eyes indicated he meant it.

7.

LIFE ON DEATH ROW

Gacy pointed me toward the vending machine where I waited behind a petite older woman dressed in what looked like minister's garb. After buying snacks and Diet Cokes for all of us, I turned to head back to the cubicle.

Along the way, I heard a deep voice say, "Miss. Can I talk to you?"

I looked across the center walkway and saw a huge African American inmate standing next to the tiny minister who had been at the vending machine. For some reason, I heard my mother warning me not to talk to strangers. I stifled a laugh. This was certainly the place to honor her advice. I walked over to the couple.

The man introduced himself, "I'm Renaldo Hudson." He was 6'2" and weighed at least 300 pounds. As he shook my hand, I noticed two things. First, his palm was dripping wet as if he had just pulled it from an aquarium. The second was that his hand was so large it wrapped completely around mine and then some. His eyes were slightly unfocused as if he were on some sort of drug. "This is my minister," he said. I did not catch her name, mainly because I was intent on protecting my personal space.

One good thing about death row is that there is no guessing what crime a prisoner had committed to land himself there. The death penalty is given only for murder, so I had a good idea which one of the Ten Commandments he had violated.

"Ma'am, would you care to pray with us?" Mr. Hudson asked, looking past me to a spot on the wall behind me. "We would like to pray for John and all of us."

How could I say no? Not being much of a believer in things religious, I certainly didn't think it would do any harm to ask for divine intervention given Gacy's situation.

I put down my vending snacks, sat down with this gigantic, convicted murderer and this tiny woman of God, held their hands, bowed my head, and listened to a short prayer in which Renaldo Hudson asked God to help guide John Wayne Gacy through his troubles to a better place and for all of the inmates at Menard to find God and recognize Jesus Christ as their savior. Amen.

I wished Mr. Hudson the best, nodded to his clergy, and returned to Gacy and Greg.

Renaldo Hudson was on death row for the brutal and senseless murder of an elderly carpenter. His upbringing was horrible and violent. After some bad conduct while on death row, Renaldo Hudson found religion and became one of the most rehabilitated model inmates in all of Illinois' history.

In September 2020, after 37 years in prison and nine years after an Illinois governor commuted the sentences of all death row inmates, Hudson was released from prison without objection by the States Attorney or the victim's family and he devoted his life to ministry, education, and community organization.

Returning from such an unexpected and intimate experience, I sat down across from Gacy and gave him his treats, which he deftly unwrapped, handcuffs be damned. He quickly polished off the junk food and washed it down with Diet Coke.

Greg nodded to me. It was time to talk business. We asked about the lawsuits the State of Illinois had brought against him invoking the rarely used law that required inmates to pay for the cost of incarceration if they had the means to do so. We had read the lawsuit and the press surrounding it. It was clear the Director of Prisons greatly disliked the publicity Gacy received by selling paintings and hosting a 900 number that people called to hear the inmate's voice professing his innocence. Most people think that the Son of Sam laws prohibit convicts from profiting from their celebrity or crimes. Those laws were passed in the 1970s but were stricken down by courts holding that even convicted inmates have First Amendment rights of expression. The Illinois "room and board" law that was being used was the State's back door to achieve the same result without violating the Constitution.

We asked why he wanted to fight this civil lawsuit when he had a more serious problem pending—like execution by lethal injection.

Gacy's first response was that upon his death he wanted to leave whatever assets he had to his family. This is what he wanted us to hear. He then told us the real reason.

"Fuck the State. Why should I pay to live in this shit hole?"

As is the case with many inmates, their only pastime is their appeals and other litigation they might have. It keeps them occupied and gives them the right to have library privileges and attorney visits. I think he enjoyed being the subject of the State's legal ire and wanted to have something else to do other than think about his impending execution.

Gacy asked us how we would defend the suit. We threw around some ideas. We could argue that he had no money from which to pay the assessed fee. Any money he had earned from selling his artwork was already given to family members. We also suggested a countersuit from the playbook: The Best Defense is a Good Offense. We could countersue the State arguing that conditions at Menard were so horrid that any money Gacy owed for room and board should be offset by the damages caused to him by having to live in such deplorable conditions. Gacy liked that one.

Greg suggested that we could also use this lawsuit to delay the execution. The contention would be, if the execution were not punishment enough and the State was also required to sue him for his last dollar, the least it could do was to delay it until after the lawsuit was resolved.

"Now you're talking," he said with a crooked grin.

Gacy seemed happy with our proposed strategy and was angling for us to handle the litigation. But something about the whole thing did not sit right with me. We were not being asked to handle his death penalty issues because he already had two very well-qualified death penalty lawyers.

John Greenlees and David Keefe were the state of the art when it came to death penalty experience, knowledge, and moral conviction. It just seemed wrong to donate our time to handle a money matter for a serial killer. The issues were not important and were not meaningful enough to set a precedent that would affect other inmates down the line. If we were going to handle a case "pro bono," which in Latin means "for the good," the cause should be a much better one than this. I put aside these thoughts knowing that Greg and I had a six-hour ride home to discuss it.

Having finished our conversation about the civil lawsuit, we chatted socially for some time, asking Gacy questions about life on death row and gossiping about fellow inmates. He told us that there were certain guys "you just stayed the fuck away from." He nodded his head toward the entrance to the room "Like that guy over there. He stabbed me about ten years ago."

Wondering who was deemed to be dangerous by a man with 33 murders under his belt, I turned to see a prisoner of small stature enter the bullpen. He was a light-skinned black man with thick eyeglasses.

"Henry Brisbon. That guy's nuts."

Considering the source of this assessment, a chill went down my spine. I looked over at the "I-57 Murderer" standing there in the flesh. I was very familiar with the case. In 1973, a woman was forced off the interstate not far from Chicago by a car carrying four men including Brisbon, a convicted rapist. He pointed a shotgun at her, ordered her to strip, and as she begged for her life, thrust the barrel of his gun into her vagina and fired. After watching her agonize for several minutes, he finished her off.

Less than an hour later, he stopped another car, this time with a young couple in it. They begged for mercy because they were engaged to be married in six months. Brisbon made them kiss and then shot them in the back of their heads.

He was sentenced to 1,000 to 3,000 years. Not being able to resist his murderous tendencies while in prison, Brisbon resourcefully sharpened a soup ladle and stabbed a fellow inmate to death. For that, he earned the right to join the elite killers here on death row. If those acts didn't make good old Henry a walking testimonial for capital punishment, he stayed busy by starting a prison riot, trying to escape by strangling a guard, trashing a courtroom during a hearing, hitting a warden with a broom handle, and attacking 15 inmates. Gacy was one of them. Ten years earlier, Brisbon had stabbed him in the arm for no apparent reason.

And there he was, all 5'9" inches of him, walking over to introduce himself.

I didn't expect to meet any Boy Scouts on this visit, but I did not bank on meeting one of the most terrifying Illinois criminals of all time. Compared to Brisbon whose life was one continuous wild crime spree, Gacy seemed gentlemanly and tame.

"Hey, Henry. Meet my lawyers, Karen and Greg."

Brisbon did not make eye contact with any of us.

"Better be some good ones, John. You gonna need some real Perry Masons." He chuckled and strutted away toward an older man in a wrinkled suit who appeared to be a lawyer. The man looked up and nodded to us as if to say, "Good luck with that case."

Back at you, I thought.

I learned later, in 2013, that while asserting his claim for clemency, Brisbon told all who would listen that if he wasn't granted a reprieve, he would cut off the prosecutor's genitals and shove them up his rectum, those words not necessarily being the actual ones he used.

...

About an hour later, a loud voice announced that lunch was served. Gacy jumped to his feet and returned with three trays balanced precariously on his arms and cuffed hands. He proudly set two of them down in front of us.

I had a blue-collar upbringing and was not fancy about my food, but what was on this tray looked like something my cat would cover. A gelatinous glob of some kind of ground meat covered with unnaturally white mashed potatoes dominated the plate. There were lima beans, three pieces of white bread, and two pints of "orange drink." The best I could say about the lunch was that it appeared to be "hearty."

Gacy lost no time and dug right in like there was no tomorrow, which for him was pretty much true. I was wondering if I should push the food around my plate and make it look like I was eating it or just offer it to Gacy right from the beginning telling him I was on a diet.

"John," Greg said, politely forking his lima beans, the least offensive of the food array, "this is amazing. I had no idea we would be served lunch. Who pays for this?"

He explained that prison etiquette dictated that when one inmate had guests, other inmates would volunteer to give up their lunches and when the other inmates had guests, the courtesy would be reciprocated. Pretty nice and cooperative, I thought. Honor among murderers. Who said there's no such thing as a free lunch?

"Just curious, John, who gave up his lunch for me? I oughta thank him."

Without missing a beat, he answered, "Charles Albanese."

Greg and I looked at each other and then at Gacy. Charles Albanese was on death row for poisoning three of his family members and attempting to poison another—with two pounds of arsenic.

Gacy suddenly burst out laughing causing food to project out of his mouth. In a second, we were all doubled over laughing. Despite the seriousness of this man's crimes and the dire legal position he was in, John Wayne Gacy had a killer sense of humor.

8.

EXITING THE PIT

During a prison visit, time stands still. No, it goes backward.

During our time at Menard, we had repeatedly glanced at our empty wrists out of habit, having stowed our watches in the prison lockers. It wasn't until 3 p.m. that we were finally able to extricate ourselves from Gacy's grip on us. Given the monotony of the days for these inmates, it is understandable that he wanted to stretch out our visit with him. Each time we gave signals—some not so subtle—that we intended to leave, he insisted on continuing our conversation. When we finally parted company, our day was already 12 hours long with a six-hour drive ahead of us.

After you visit a prison, you are physically and mentally exhausted. Only after walking out the door do you understand the stress you were under and how your psyche has been affected by the depressing conditions. The idea that people commit such heinous crimes requiring them to be locked away like animals is something we know about in the abstract, but to immerse yourself in that world is like the difference between reading about the English Channel and swimming it.

We retrieved our belongings and bade farewell to the desk guard who didn't look up to acknowledge our attempt at politeness. Normally I would be pissy about an employee not having the courtesy of doing his job with a modicum of cordiality. If you work at Target, this makes some sense, but it's hard to blame a maximum-security prison guard for having a bad attitude. If I worked in this place, I would need antidepressants just to get step foot on the job each morning.

We trudged to the car in silence. How could it be that so much had changed since the time we arrived? The curiosity-driven road trip that carried no obligations or expectations presented some undefined, serious, and disturbing issues we had to consider.

The sunlight was fading but we still had at least two hours before sunset. Greg and I agreed to make the most of the dwindling daylight and make a beeline for Chicago with the probability that we would stop somewhere along the way for dinner and a cheap motel.

For the first 45 minutes, we wound our way back to the main highway on narrow rural roads. The farther away we got from Menard, Gacy, and death row, the more my energy was restored.

9.

FROM THE BEGINNING

I began my career at a large, prestigious Chicago firm where along with 200 other attorneys, I was tasked with representing large insurance companies that insured banks and savings and loans during what was known as the Savings and Loan Crisis.

Effectively starting as a slow-moving disaster during the 1980s, over 1,600 such institutions failed nationwide due to excessive extensions of credit, deregulation, speculation, fraud, and the terrible sense on the part of savings and loans that the taxpayer would foot the bill. This resulted in $160 billion in losses at the banks, $132 billion that was paid by taxpayers. In a review of the incident by Calavita, Pontell and Tillman, et al. in the book, *Big Money Crime*, "The savings and loan debacle involved a series of white-collar crimes unparalleled in American history."

Many individuals, small businesses, and family farms failed as a knock-on effect, forcing people into poverty with some resorting to suicide. Before the crisis, people generally trusted bankers to work in their best interests. The lies that facilitated the severity of the crisis left a bad taste in many taxpayers' mouths.

In light of all that, my job was essentially to find a way to deny coverage to these businesses that paid astronomical insurance premiums for protection from these losses. It rubbed me the wrong way to work long hours six days a week to achieve results I did not like. Like so many people, I kept the job because I had sizeable student loans that needed paying. The bonus lesson was I also learned to analyze complicated insurance policies to find ways of obtaining insurance coverage for people who needed it. In short, I learned to play for the offense by first playing for the defense.

Throughout my legal career, I made a point of taking on insurance companies with the hope of making up for the part I played as a young lawyer in denying coverage. After two years, I left the large firm to get more hands-on experience when it came to making arguments, taking depositions, and trying cases. (In the large firm, the monetary stakes were so high that young lawyers like me would never have been assigned such important tasks.)

Unfortunately, I went from the fire into the legal frying pan in joining a small firm run by lawyers whose real talents were sexually harassing women and pushing their associates to overbill clients.

I became the victim of the former at the hands of the founding partner, who wanted me to parade in front of male clients in short skirts and meet them for meals where they could "get to know me better." He was also inappropriately flirting with me, having me stay late to "discuss cases" in the hopes I'd let my guard down. His behavior was humiliating because I had come to learn and practice law, while he made a mockery of it.

Being young and naive, I tried to placate and deflect instead of standing up for myself and leaving the firm: sexual harassment isn't based on attraction or care but strictly on power and control.

Although I would handle the issue differently now, I was young and was focused on making money to support myself. I tolerated this disgusting behavior only until I could land another job. The experience haunted me for years, but as is common, every experience serves you well later in life. I have since represented many women who have been harassed and discriminated against in the workplace. I am proud to say that I later handled an important appeal that reversed Illinois law in favor of women who have been sexually assaulted at their jobs. I have made it a point to hire and mentor hundreds of women throughout my career.

Soured by these two initial law firm experiences, I strongly considered leaving the profession. To pay the bills, I took a job part-time in a suite of lawyers at the historic LaSalle Bank Building. The job also allowed me to earn a decent wage while working for a startup business that provided exercise equipment and management to corporate fitness centers. It combined my love of athletics with my desire to be part of something positive and productive. I negotiated and drafted the client's contracts, helped market his business, and handled his litigation. I adored the work and the client, who is still a friend to this day.

At this time, I met the man who would become my partner and then my husband, Greg Adamski.

Greg was a tenant in the office suite, a solo practitioner. He was a force of nature. I had heard from others in the suite that he had been the youngest lawyer ever to make partner in the mega-firm of Winston & Strawn. He was brilliant, aggressive, and a workaholic. Greg was 6'1", broad-shouldered, and although he had about 30 pounds of extra weight, he carried it well, as tall men in well-tailored suits can. With a full head of blonde hair and riveting blue eyes, he was handsome and charismatic.

Greg told the story that, when he met the dancer Mikhail Baryshnikov at a benefit for the ballet in New York City, Greg leaned over and said, "People say I look like Mikhail" to which Baryshnikov responded in his Russian accent, "No. No. Two Mikhails."

Although I was never introduced to Greg formally, I saw him in the office: a whirling dervish of energy, laughter, and mischief. I asked other lawyers about him, and they told me, "That guy is crazy. Brilliant, but crazy."

One Friday in late August, I went to the office kitchen needing caffeine. Greg was there, tie loosened around his neck, pouring himself a cup of coffee into a Chicago Cubs mug. He held out his hand. "I'm Greg. I should quit drinking coffee because I don't need more energy. Are you the lawyer who worked for the big firm? Where did you go to law school?"

I was impressed that he already knew a little something about me. Although his eyes were intense and piercing, behind them was an undefined sadness. He told me he was trying a case and needed some help with research. "You can help me, right?"

Whoa, I thought. *This guy doesn't even know who I am, and he assumes I am going to jump right in and help him.*

He turned out to be right. Most people could not refuse Greg's requests, and I was no different.

I followed him into his office where he sat me down in front of his huge executive desk. He explained that the case going to trial was an injunction action, meaning the client was asking the court for something other than money to stop a former employee from stealing business. The client was an importer of flowers who flew thousands of dollars of product into the country daily from South America to the Midwest where he had a sales force set up to sell to retailers.

One of the salesmen had left the company and was actively competing using customer lists and proprietary pricing information. This violated the non-compete clause he had signed upon taking the job. These cases are very important to companies that have long-term customer relationships because one employee can strip that company of its business in a matter of months if left unrestrained. Trial was scheduled to start the following week, and Greg needed me to research the issue of what constitutes a "near-permanent customer relationship." Only businesses with those types of customers are entitled to enforce a non-compete clause and obtain an order enjoining or stopping the employee from competing. I told him that I would come in during the weekend to do it. I could use the money, and it seemed like an interesting assignment.

Early the next morning, after my six-mile run on the beautiful Chicago lakefront path, I headed to the office's small and un-airconditioned law library. Sipping a Diet Coke, I sat for hours poring over pages and pages of cases, taking notes, and making copies of decisions that had facts similar to ours and favorable to our arguments.

Back in those days, there were computer databases like Westlaw and Lexis, but only large law firms could afford access to them. So, for the small practitioners, research was a physical exercise that required lugging books back and forth from the shelves. After several hours of toiling in the muggy library, I was sweaty and exhausted. Grabbing my file stuffed with the relevant cases, I headed down to the office where I found Greg sitting at his desk, smoking with one hand, typing with the other, and talking on the speakerphone. Greg could only perform tasks well if he were doing at least three at the same time. I now see this as adult Attention Deficit Disorder.

We discussed my research results. For probably the first time in my four years of practice, another lawyer listened to me and it made me feel so validated. He drilled me. What were the top three most persuasive opinions? What was the best opposing argument? What was the counterargument? What evidence should be elicited from witnesses? As I answered, Greg nodded, and after I stopped talking, he said simply, "Do you want to try this case with me? Make the opening?"

"No" didn't seem to be an option. And so that is how I tried my very first case.

In the Chicago court, injunctions are tried to the bench, meaning by a judge. Ours was a female judge who liked the fact that Greg had chosen a young woman as his trial partner. For years afterward, we used the male/female partnership to our advantage, some clients and judges preferring a man and some preferring a woman.

Greg was better at pushing and demanding. I was better at client handholding and negotiation. I made the opening statement methodically, giving the judge a roadmap of the witnesses and expected testimony. I also took control of the voluminous documents that were entered into evidence, my organizational skills being stronger than Greg's.

But the best part of this trial was watching a great lawyer in action. Greg's courtroom talent was breathtaking. He commanded the courtroom. He dominated everyone in it. He was smart, charming, down-to-Earth, and persuasive beyond belief. He was fearless and a little reckless. He took chances, but they always seemed to come out in his favor. He framed the facts in a way that you could not imagine any other result than the one he was demanding. You almost felt sorry for his opponent.

We were working 13-hour days and were adrenalized by the pressures of trial. Greg would always say, "Trying cases is the most fun you can have with your clothes on." I understand what he meant. Trials force you to be at the top of your game. You must be prepared, alert, creative, and instinctive. You are a scholar and a showman. With so much at stake, trials are exhilarating.

After five solid days in court followed by long evenings of intense preparation, the judge announced she was ready to rule. We waited anxiously as she gathered her notes and her written ruling.

To our delight, the judge granted our injunction, issuing a stern order that the employee immediately cease competing and return all proprietary information within hours.

As we listened to the judge's findings, Greg and I knocked knees together in a discrete courtroom "high five." There would be a subsequent trial on the issue of monetary damages caused by the breach of the restrictive covenant, but for now, our work was done, and we were the victors. We stood up, thanked the judge for her attention, and shook hands with our opposing counsel. In the hallway outside the courtroom, the client threw his arms around us and thanked us profusely. There was nothing left to do but share a celebratory drink together.

Chicago is a veritable playground when it comes to eating and drinking. With very little discussion, we chose the bar at the Italian Village, a charming landmark restaurant a few blocks away from the courthouse. Greg and I had a mutual liking for the old-style Chicago restaurants and agreed that the "IV" was the best. We also loved the story of its origin. The founder, Alfredo Capitanini, emigrated from Florence to Chicago and worked as a cook and dishwasher to save money to start his own restaurant. Opened in 1927, the Village soon became a mecca for workers, shoppers, entertainers, and mafiosos, including Al Capone. Led down the stairs by Hans, the tall, handsome Turkish maître d', we descended to the bar in the lower level tucked away in the corner of the cozy, dark dining room.

For hours we sat and talked. Despite Greg's enormous intellect and talents, he had been going through a difficult time. He was open and honest about his problems and seemed relieved he could talk to me about them. Like too many affluent professionals at that time, he suffered from a previous cocaine addiction, which, he confessed, was costly to his pocketbook, marriage, and professional life. Although I abhor drugs and had never even smoked pot, I admired Greg's honesty and determination that he was not going back to that dark time in his life.

He would later tell me and everyone who would listen that this conversation saved his life; he thought he had destroyed so many things that he was unsure he could come out of it. He said seeing me, young, healthy, and ambitious, reminded him of who he used to be and could be again. He said I represented life when he wanted death. Perhaps he was exaggerating my importance in his recovery, but if I was an unknowing lifesaver, I am glad. It is a great lesson: Your random acts of kindness and empathy may help people in ways you will never know.

After a couple of hours at the bar, we moved to the dining area and supped on stuffed artichokes, minestrone, and large plates of pasta. I laughed as I listened to what I would later call "Greg Stories," which were largely true although slightly amplified. As he would often say, "Never let the truth get in the way of a good story." Full of wine, Italian food, and quite a bit of personal knowledge about each other, we parted ways in separate cabs.

Two months later, after working on several cases together, Greg made me an offer: "Be my partner." I told him no. I did not want a structured relationship because I was still soured a bit on the practice of law, had only known Greg for a short time, and was unsure how stable Greg would be in the long run, given his personal baggage. I longed for regularity and the ability to meet my financial obligations.

He told me he would split all profits with me. "Fifty percent of nothing is still nothing," I said.

Then one day, Greg walked into the office with a huge grin on his face. He threw a small box on my desk. It was a set of business cards that read, "Adamski & Conti." I was so angry I left the office for a walk. *Who does this man think he is? Trying to force me into a partnership with him?* I have never liked to be controlled, and I felt this was a move to dominate. I cooled off and returned to the office.

"What you did is wrong," I told him firmly.

"Okay. I can change the firm name to Conti & Adamski." I smirked.

"Give it a test run, Karen," Greg said softly. "If it doesn't work, no harm." As a wise bard once said, "The best men are molded out of faults …"

I was determined to maintain my relationship with Greg Adamski, and if he wanted me to work with him for the time being, I was ready and willing. I knew I could help him right himself, and I also knew he could teach me valuable lessons about being a lawyer.

Later, our relationship took a romantic turn but that also came with its complications. Greg was 14 years older than me. He had been married twice, and the second one was still in the process of demolition. He also had a son who lived full-time with him. He was not in the best financial position and was trying to resuscitate his client base and professional life. Along with the past drug addiction, these facts did not bode well. But I liked him and respected him.

As I look back, I realize that not all great relationships start with immediate fireworks and physical attraction. Some of them start slowly with kindness, respect, and loyalty and later develop into a healthy, mutually loving, and committed lifetime partnership. That is what happened with Greg.

10.

DECISIONS DECISIONS

There was much to discuss on our return trip to Chicago from our inaugural death row visit.

The first thing I said to Greg was, "You know, Greg. Of all things we talked about, we didn't once talk about his crimes, his guilt or innocence."

"It seemed like it wasn't the right thing to do. We were like dogs sniffing each other," Greg offered.

"Maybe you were sniffing, but I was too busy worrying about an attack from one of the rabid ones ..."

Greg suggested that to pass the time, I read from *Buried Dreams* to review everything we could about the crimes and the trial. I knew that Greg wanted to occupy his perpetually overactive mind to find some clarity about the decisions we both knew we soon needed to make. Skimming through my Gacy guide, I summarized the sordid details of the crimes that condemned the man to death.

On the night he was arrested, he gave the police an exceptionally detailed account of the murders. His lawyers asked him not to, but he insisted. He told them more the next day and more the following day. He actually drew a map of where the bodies were buried, which turned out to be amazingly accurate. Thereafter and until his execution, Gacy contended he knew nothing about the murders except one, which was a boy he picked up at a Greyhound bus station, had sex with, and then killed—according to him in self-defense after the boy attacked him.

From the initial account and the police investigation, this is what we know about the rest of the crimes. Gacy's victims were either men he knew as employees or men he randomly picked up at bars, parks, and gay hangouts such as Bughouse Square, a park on the north side of Chicago. He usually lured the man to his home, offered him a job with his construction company, and then plied him with alcohol and drugs in exchange for sex. Some victims were grabbed by force, others conned into believing Gacy (who often carried a sheriff's badge and had spotlights on his black Oldsmobile) was a policeman.

Once he had gained the trust of his prey, he would display a pair of handcuffs to demonstrate a magic trick that entailed him cuffing himself and then escaping the cuffs. He would then offer to show the victim how to perform the trick. With his victim manacled and unable to free himself, he would say words to the effect, "The trick is, you have to have the key." Gacy referred to the devious act as the "handcuff trick."

Once his victims were restrained, he raped and tortured them. He often began by sitting on the victim's chest and forcing him to perform oral sex. He would shackle their ankles and inflict acts of torture including burning them with cigars and making them imitate a horse as he sat on their back and pulled on makeshift reins wrapped around their throats. After sodomizing them, he would continue to violate their body cavity with foreign objects such as dildos and prescription bottles. Some victims were dragged to the bathtub where Gacy would drown them to the point of death and then revive them repeatedly so he could repeat his sexual assault.

He typically murdered his victims by placing a rope tourniquet around their necks before progressively tightening the rope with a hammer handle. This "rope trick" was the final trick. Occasionally, the victim convulsed for an hour or two before dying, although several victims died by asphyxiation from cloth gags stuffed deep into their throats.

Gacy usually stored the victims' bodies under his bed for

up to 24 hours before burying them in the crawlspace, where he periodically poured acid or lime to hasten the decomposition of the body.

After the crawlspace was filled, he buried other men on other parts of his property and drove others to the nearby Des Plaines River where he dumped them from a bridge.

A few times, he killed two boys in one night.

Once, he killed three.

During these murders, he took prodigious amounts of drugs and drank excessive amounts of alcohol. He always awoke the next morning, went to work on time, and was productive at his job.

On December 11, 1978, Gacy committed his last murder, that of 15-year-old Robert Piest. He agreed to meet Piest at a pharmacy in Des Plaines to discuss employing the boy to do some construction work for his company. When Piest's mother came to pick him up to celebrate her birthday with the family, she was told he was talking to someone about a job. He was never seen alive again.

Distraught, Mrs. Piest filed a missing person's report and the focus was on Gacy. A routine background check revealed an outstanding sexual battery charge against him in Chicago and a prison sentence in Iowa for the sodomy of a 15-year-old boy. Search warrants were issued and the rest is history.

We traveled for some time in silence. I thought: *Gacy is bad news. If capital punishment is to be used for anyone, this is the guy.* But I just could not get on board with the idea that the state was going to strap him down and kill him. He was locked up, of no harm to anyone, and was rotting away at a hellish prison. In my mind, this man's immoral conduct did not justify a premeditated killing by a civilized government.

I couldn't contain myself any longer. "Greg, we have to do something. We have to do more than just handle this bullshit civil suit. They're going to kill this guy. And then the rest of them are next, and some also are innocent."

"What are you suggesting?" He knew full well.

"We have to get in on the death penalty defense. We have to figure out a way to work with Greenlees and Keefe and help them try to save Gacy's life."

"Karen, we weren't asked to handle the death case. Greenlees and Keefe don't want us to intrude on what they're doing. We have no experience at this level. Oh, and we are a two-person firm with no resources. This is going to be one shit-show."

"Have you ever been asked to do anything this important?" Appealing to Greg's sizeable legal ego, I added, "And when has not having done something before stopped you from throwing your hat in the ring? Could adding two legal minds and willing hands hurt the cause? What's the worst that could happen? Gacy is executed?"

Silence.

I knew at this point I did not have to convince Greg. He was sparring with me to convince himself of what he already knew. If Gacy and his current lawyers agreed, we would soon be on the team … with very little time to suit up.

11.

HIRED BY A KILLER

Energized by our decision, we decided to drive all the way back home that evening. With stops only for coffee, bathroom breaks, and a greasy omelet at a family-owned diner outside of Effingham, we pulled up to our home a little after 1 a.m. My cat noisily greeted me at the door, letting me know he had missed his evening feeding. "You think *you* had a hard day," I said. That and a scoop of cat food seemed to satisfy him.

Greg and I were out of words and energy. We dropped our bags and the next thing I remember was awakening at 8 a.m. with the sun streaming through the bedroom window and an empty pillow next to me. The sunlight cast a spotlight on my clothes and briefcase contents, which looked like they had been thrown from a pottery wheel onto the bedroom floor. As I picked up my suit, I had an urge to throw it in the garbage. Being in a prison makes you long for a hot shower and a new set of clothing. Even then you feel as if you can never come clean again.

As I shuffled sleepily down the stairs, I smelled coffee and toast.

Greg was sitting in the sunny kitchen, drinking coffee and reading the newspaper. "Ready for some cereal, killer?"

"Funny. Where's Rik?"

Rik was Greg's 14-year-old son from his first marriage. Greg had obtained full custody of him several years back when he was a partner at the mega-firm Winston and Strawn. At that time, big firm male lawyers like Greg would rarely be awarded custody of their children, so Greg treasured the fact that he got to raise him.

"Rik left for school. He had to be there early."

Probably not. He was likely smoking pot and playing hacky sack with his friends before his first class. I grabbed a mug of black coffee and plopped down across from Greg.

"So what's the plan?" Greg knew I was talking about Gacy.

"John has taken a real liking to you, so I think you should be the one to talk to him about us joining the death squad. I'll talk to the capital lawyers and tell them we want to come on board."

Flattered that a serial killer thought I was the cat's meow, I was pretty sure that he would agree to let us join. Why not? If we were working for free, the more the merrier. Greg had the tougher job—to get the death squad to approve. Greenlees and Keefe might be bent out of shape about having two for-profit lawyers with no capital punishment experience joining the team. They seemed to be "true believers" and were likely to think we were improperly motivated or inexperienced. They also might think that we would try to usurp their litigation strategies.

Lawyers largely have big egos and experienced lawyers justifiably want to control how a case is handled. Greg, who had an inordinate overabundance of aggressive genes, would have to resist the urge to dominate, agree to take a back seat to these lawyers, and follow their lead. I knew I could play nice because I had no experience at all in a case of this magnitude and any role I would have would not be as leader of the pack. Plus, I think women generally have less of a desire to call the shots and a better ability to proceed by consensus.

Knowing the plan, we agreed to shower, dress, and start an important day at work.

...

Connecting with a prisoner by phone is not easy. Rules often require you to be on an approved list for making and taking calls and you must have a prison "account." When an inmate calls, it is collect and must be to a landline, not a cell phone, not that we had the luxury of a cell phone in 1993.

When we left Menard the day before, we told Gacy to call us the next morning at 11 a.m. to discuss moving forward with the defense of the civil suit. Promptly at 10:58 a.m., my secretary came into my office to tell me that Mr. John Gacy was on the phone. She had a strange, confused look on her face and her eyes were open wide. Although she knew we had gone to visit him the day before, she seemed stunned that she had just spoken to a notorious killer. I would learn this was a common phenomenon. As horrified as people were about him and his monstrous deeds, they were fascinated by having contact with him. I heard my secretary say, "Mr. Gacy, I will put you through to Ms. Conti." We were certainly formal here.

I picked up the phone. "Hi, John."

"Dollface."

This was the second time he used that nickname with me. As we were parting yesterday, he stood up, shook Greg's hand, and expressed his appreciation that Greg and I had come to see him. He then turned to me, took both my hands in his, and said with a wink, "Especially you, Dollface." He would refer to me with that term of endearment throughout the time I knew him. It seemed so 1930s Humphrey Bogart.

We chatted for five minutes, making small talk. When he was engaged in these kinds of conversations, Gacy was charming, intelligent, and affable. This is common for sociopaths. They are normally glib and engaging, which allows them to manipulate people and fool them into thinking that they are harmless. I knew I needed to get to the meat of the conversation. I told him that we would like to help him with his civil litigation (not true), but we also wanted to help him in a more meaningful way and that was to assist in representing him in his death row appeals. He did not react as I thought he would. He became argumentative.

"I already have two death penalty lawyers. I want you to focus on the prison's lawsuit against me! That's your forte, not the death stuff."

I calmly told him that the State of Illinois was getting ready to unleash all of its formidable resources to make sure that the May 10 execution would go as planned. There were probably 20 states attorneys and attorneys general who were manning the canons at the state capitol and in Chicago to make sure that the appeals—from the state to federal to U.S. Supreme Court—were handled quickly and aggressively. I knew these lawyers oftentimes started writing briefs way before any appeal was filed so that when the inmate filed last-minute appeals, the state could make a few tweaks to the already-drafted response and get it on file within the hour.

"John, you could use a few more good lawyers. It couldn't hurt. Greenlees and Keefe are great but they could use our backup. We have brains, a small staff, and resources that could help them and you."

I thought to myself: *Is this crazy? I am arguing with one of the most despised men in the world, trying to convince him that Greg and I—two reputable lawyers—should be allowed to donate what would amount to hundreds of thousands of dollars of free legal work to try to save his life.*

The answer should have simply been, "Yes. Thanks." But Gacy had a belligerent streak that I would learn frequently worked against his best interests. I kept thinking: try to empathize. What is it that he wants here? Respect. To show that he is smarter than everyone. Control—something he lacks sitting in that rat hole of a prison cell 23 hours a day awaiting death. *Give him what he wants,* Karen.

"John, you're right. You're in control here. I don't want to join a team unless the captain thinks I'm going to help win the game. I know what kind of businessman you are. When you were on the outside, you always put together a good team of employees." (When you weren't murdering them.) "Of course, I will defer to you, but what do you think of this plan? Greg will be the one to help Greenlees and Keefe with the heavy lifting on the appeals and court appearances. I will be your face when it comes to talking to the press ... the one to advocate for you against the death penalty. I will explain to the world why you should not be executed. I will be your PR person. It's your call."

Gacy paused for a moment. "Will we sell T-shirts? Free Gacy?"

Having already spent several hours with this man, I knew he was kidding. This was his way of changing his mind and deflecting attention from the fact that he was doing so.

"Yes, John. T-shirts and clown noses. Do we have a deal?"

"All right, Dollface. You can have your way with me."

"Is that what all the girls say, John?"

"Welcome aboard."

As if this were the Love Boat and not the Titanic.

I hung up the phone and bolted into Greg's office. He was just getting off a conference call with the death penalty lawyers. I told him that Gacy had agreed to us representing him. Greg told me that, as expected, Greenlees and Keefe were not thrilled about us joining in but acquiesced because it was clear that they could use our help on this monumental task.

"Ready for this, Dollface?" Greg asked.

...

Many people have criticized me for representing John Wayne Gacy and will continue to do so for the rest of my life.

There are people—including many who are reading this—who believe that because I fought Gacy's execution, I am a bad person and I somehow condone the conduct that put him behind bars. Let's just say this plainly: I do not believe that torturing, raping, and killing innocent young men and boys is in any way acceptable behavior. I affirmatively believe that the Gacys of the world belong in jail forever. He was an immoral, dangerous person and the only place for him was behind a solid, locked door with no possibility of ever spending time in society. And one more thing: Had he killed my son or brother, I could have killed him with my own hands.

As a lawyer, we do not make those judgments. We are

obligated and wired to advocate zealously and almost blindly for our clients. I have represented completely innocent people, but mostly not. Before I met Gacy, I had represented many clients whose conduct I abhorred. I continue to do so to this day. I have represented billion-dollar insurance companies that have denied coverage to deserving widows, men who have beaten their wives, companies that have knowingly sold cancer-causing products, women who have abandoned their newborns, young people who have abused animals, surely on their way to committing even worse crimes, and conmen who have defrauded the innocent. Lawyers look at every client as somebody with an unchangeable set of facts they need to contend with to get them the best result possible.

In the case of Gacy, I tried to stop his execution. His morality or lack thereof had nothing to do with it. When you are a lawyer, you do not make assessments as to whether someone is a good or bad person or did or did not do the right thing. It's like being a doctor. If an overweight smoker and drinker comes to the emergency room having a heart attack, the doctor does not say, "Wow, you abused your body. You are not deserving of my medical attention." The doctor takes the person as he is and goes to work on fixing the problem as effectively as possible, trying to save the patient's life. I do not have the option to judge a person before doing my job. That is for judges and juries and, if you believe in a higher power, the man (or woman) upstairs.

People also say, "How can you advocate for a result that is not justice?" Lawyers are not in charge of making sure the world comes out the way it should or the way *we* think it should. We can only advocate for our clients. Our criminal justice system is a very good one. When I am defending an accused, I firmly believe that if I do my job, the prosecutor does his job, the judge does her job, and the jury members are impartial and follow their oath, then justice will usually be served.

12.

GEARING UP FOR BATTLE

Gacy was at the end of his legal road. For the past 14 years, his conviction and death sentence were appealed numerous times in both state and federal courts. Once those appeals were lost and the execution date was set by the governor, he was essentially out of traditional avenues for legal recourse.

At this point, we were forced to get creative. We had to attack everything about the conviction and sentence we could — matters that were already raised in the hopes that a new judge would change the outcome, new issues related to new evidence if any, and the method of execution which could at least delay it for a few days or weeks. Affecting other cases in the future by setting a precedent was even more compelling.

Once we reviewed the appellate briefs and court opinions, we discussed our plan of action. Greenlees and Keefe had already given much thought to the strategy, and we were on board with it. Some appeals would reiterate what had been argued. We would file additional appeals again contending the jury instructions were confusing when it came to sentencing. We would argue ineffective assistance of counsel in that the trial lawyer did not put on evidence that would have mitigated against the death penalty.

The new, creative arguments had to do with the method of execution. We would argue that the lethal injection machine in Illinois violated the Eighth Amendment prohibition against cruel and unusual punishment. The death penalty in and of itself had long been held to be constitutional as it was in active use well before the Constitution and amendments were ratified.

The issue was the use of Illinois' death machine which had been sold to them by a disreputable charlatan named Fred Leuchter. Neither a physician nor an engineer, Leuchter was a traveling salesman who sold implements for killing people. You've heard of *Death of a Salesman*? Well, Leuchter was the Salesman of Death. He was also a vocal Holocaust denier, having published articles and testifying in court that there were no gas chambers at Auschwitz. As a fan and student of the Nazis, Leuchter used their research on methods of killing Jews during World War II to design his death device. Leuchter's past experience also included being charged with misrepresentation in Massachusetts for telling a prison's administration that he was an engineer and for practicing engineering without a license. He was accused of running a "death row shakedown" in which he threatened to testify for the defense in capital cases if he was not given the contract for his services by that state. Finally, he was once deported from Europe for denying the Holocaust, which is illegal in several countries.

Colorful resume aside, the Leuchter lethal injection machine simply did not work. It had failed when used in other states and had failed in the execution of Charles Walker, who was the last person executed in Illinois in 1990. The chairman of the anesthesia department at Northwestern University Medical School predicted the machine would paralyze a condemned criminal, and far from being humane, this paralysis would merely stop the prisoner from screaming at the "extreme pain in the form of a severe burning sensation" caused by the potassium chloride injection.

We planned to gather all evidence that the machine would not work and present it to the state court, asking that the execution be delayed until Illinois found a more merciful way to kill its condemned prisoners, which was hopefully never.

Another argument was that putting someone to death is a medical procedure and as such must be performed by a physician, according to the law. Doctors were prohibited from taking part in an execution because it violates the Hippocratic Oath; therefore, lethal injection was illegal and could not proceed.

Finally, we would attempt to find new evidence—any new evidence that could be used to argue that Gacy deserved a new trial or at the very least a new sentencing hearing. If we could shine new light on these old crimes, perhaps the state would pause the death machine long enough to examine the issue of whether it missed new victims, perpetrators, or conspirators.

We divided up these tasks with the agreement that all the filings would be reviewed and approved by the team. Some appeals would intentionally be delayed until the last minute in hopes that the courts would be unable to decide them before the execution, buying Gacy some extra time. Greg and I were not keen on that strategy since, in our legal world, procrastination generally did not result in good outcomes. In the end, we deferred to the lawyers who had capital punishment experience.

It was decided that I would be the person spearheading the public message. I would do my best to send out the message loudly and clearly that the death penalty was wrong, even for someone like Gacy. The anti-death penalty message was a goal in and of itself to help whoever came after Gacy. I looked at it as a pool game. We were trying to get the ball in the pocket—a long shot—but if we couldn't, we were setting up the table for the next one.

13.

THE NIGHT BEFORE THE EXECUTION
May 9, 1994
11:22 p.m.

With the prison warden gone, the guards continue their nervous banter with Gacy. One would think prison employees would be used to stressful situations, but these men are visibly uncomfortable with tonight's duties. Nobody here likes executions.

They put the other inmates in a bad mood, which makes them unruly and hard to control, feeling and acting like they have nothing left to lose. Gacy had very little in common with the majority of the Stateville residents who were poor black and brown men with tortured backgrounds, most with certifiable mental illness. Their crimes paled in comparison with his. Still, nobody enjoyed seeing one of their own killed, not even the likes of John Gacy. When he was gone, the gears of the Illinois capital punishment machine would be greased.

Gacy seems to be the only one in the room who is comfortable, at ease in his surroundings. He keeps up the conversation.

"How many thrill-seekers are out there on the lawn waiting for me to die?" he asks, basking in the idea that he still commands the public's morbid interest.

"More than you killed, John," quips the tallest guard,

causing the rest of the group to chuckle nervously, welcoming the comic relief from the tension of the day. In another world, the men in this room could be sitting in a bar having beers and chatting about sports, politics, and current events. Tonight, they avoid the ultimate current event of the day: execution by lethal injection. A loud buzz interrupts the quiet chatter. A two-way radio held by one of the guards announces the final journey is about to begin.

"It's time for the rodeo," says the guard.

Gacy deadpans, "Just keep me away from the horseshit."

A noise at the entrance. The lock turns and the door opens. Three additional sheriffs appear, ready for the transport. They stare at Gacy, a criminal legend about whom books have been written and movies made.

Perhaps they are expecting to see a monster in their midst, but instead take in the normal appearance of an average Joe, a man who you would not notice at a bus stop or on a bar stool.

They firmly grasp the arms of the man of honor and lead him out of the room. They parade him down the speckled tile floors of the recently mopped hallway. The walls have been given a fresh coat of pale-yellow paint for this momentous occasion, the execution of the highest-profile inmate in the prison's history.

At the end of the corridor, the tallest guard with a mustache takes out a large set of ancient metal keys that look like they could be used to unlock a castle door. They enter a small, harshly illuminated room ...

14.

GOING SOUTH ... AGAIN

Almost immediately after Gacy became a client, he began calling our office daily. Whether this was because he was bored, lonely, scared, or because this made him feel important, we took his calls. He was like no other client in this regard.

When you represent a litigant, you must constantly be aware of boundary lines. At any given time, I represent 50 to 60 clients. I get to know them personally and consider my relationship with them to be friendly, warm, and human. This helps me advocate for their interests and empathize with their plight no matter what bad decisions or personality traits put them in that position. It also helps us through the attorney-client relationship which can become contentious and emotional. They must trust my judgment when it comes time for them to take the tough advice I may have to give them. A personal connection smooths the way.

That said, I always make sure they don't take advantage of my time, compassion, and energy. Lawyering, like most professions, is stressful. Each client feels that his case is the most important and difficult matter in their lives. If I let clients greatly infringe on my personal space, I cannot be effective for them, my other clients, or myself.

So why did I give Gacy full access to my time and attention? He had, at most, seven months to live. That finality resonated with me. How many people do you know who have a definite amount of time left? Knowing that makes you a little nicer to and more patient with that person. I also knew that Gacy was volatile. I had not yet experienced that side of him, but having read almost everything written about this man, I knew that there was rage and anger beneath his amiable surface.

Important decisions would soon need to be made, some of them of life and death magnitude, and a good connection with him would help us all through it. To the extent that you can ever truly develop a friendship with an antisocial personality, I had to make every effort to have one.

The second week in November, Gacy called the office. I always took his call first to kid with him and engage in small talk to put him in a more receptive mood. Greg tended to get right down to business, but that was not the best strategy. He needed a little schmoozing before he was ready to hear about the status of his many legal maneuvers and then to give the consent we needed to proceed.

After some playful banter about the upcoming Thanksgiving dinner at Menard, I sensed he would start angling for us to come down to visit. Sure enough.

"When are ya comin' down? I need to talk about a bunch of things with youse, and you know the prison motherfuckers are listening to our conversations."

"JW, we're really busy doing legal work for you. You know how many things we're working on." I then recounted the five motions and appeals we were researching and writing on his behalf.

"I'd meet you halfway if I could, Dollface, but the warden's not keen on the idea."

"Okay. I'll talk to the big guy." I could pass the buck with the best of them.

"I hope you're talkin' about Greg and not God. Though he probably thinks they're one and the same."

Three days later, we were on our way back to Menard. We left hours before dawn with the majority of miles traveled in complete darkness. The landscape had changed drastically in the short time since our first trip. As winter descended, the trees had disrobed themselves, exposing only their toughest parts—trunks, branches, and bark. By the time we made the next trip, a white covering of snow would likely have blanketed their skeletonized arms only to be uncovered when spring made its reluctant, Midwest appearance.

By then, Gacy's days would be numbered in double digits. We used our driving time productively, discussing and drafting documents for clients we had begun to ignore. Some of them had heard that we were representing Gacy and needed assurances that this case would not prevent us from giving them our attention.

As we sped south on I-57, Greg and I joked about how many of the drivers next to us were transporting drugs on what we called The Heroin Highway. It is well-known to Illinois state police that drugs are transported from the southern border north on this highway through Memphis, Illinois, and Chicago. From there, drugs are distributed to New York, Detroit, Los Angeles, and other cities across the country.

In the late 1980s, police pulled over a rental van and found $72 million of pure Colombian cocaine in 500 neatly wrapped bundles, making it one of the largest drug busts in Illinois history. Many years later, it was revealed that Chicago acted as the American distribution center for the vast network of the Sinaloa cartel, led by El Chapo himself, which transported billions of dollars of drugs in untold numbers of truck and train shipments, hidden among loads of vegetables, meat, and even live sheep. The police who patrol the highway receive special training on how to "spot" drug smugglers, i.e., people of Mexican descent driving beat-up vans.

Two years earlier, Greg and I handled a case for "the Hernandez Brothers" who were stopped by police on I-57 near the town of Effingham with substantial amounts of marijuana in their 25-year-old rusty station wagon. The intended recipient of this stash, a reputed drug dealer in Chicago, also charged, had hired a lawyer who contacted us promising that our fees would be paid to defend the Hernandez defendants. The gangbanger wanted to make sure these guys had a consistent and strong defense. When we arrived in Effingham to meet our clients, headlines in the local paper reported that three members of the "Hernandez Drug Cartel" had been apprehended. In a very white and rural community, this kind of pre-trial publicity did not bode well for a potential jury pool if the case were to go to trial.

When we got to the lock-up, we did not find a cartel. We found three young, poor Mexican kids who were scared out of their minds. Turns out they were migrant farm workers who lived in Juarez, Mexico, just across the Texas border. Dubbed "the world's most dangerous city," 35% of Juarez's population lives in extreme poverty—unable to meet even basic needs. Most make $50 per week as factory workers. Every summer, the three brothers would jump in their battered car and travel to dairy farms in Wisconsin, strawberry fields in North Carolina, and cantaloupe and melon farms in Indiana to labor for 12 hours a day doing back-breaking work.

Each brother brought in about $8,000 annually for this labor. On this one unfortunate occasion, they had agreed to haul an illegal crop up to Chicago for $1,000—a king's ransom that would provide support for their families for months.

After we were retained, I came up with the idea of putting together "a day in the life" video for the prosecutors and, if necessary, jurors. The goal was to show that these poor young men were not drug traffickers and should not be punished as such.

About a week later, we were on a plane to El Paso. We rented a car, picked up a Spanish-speaking videographer, and crossed the Texas border into Juarez. The city exuded danger. There were gang signs everywhere and police with machine guns driving down the streets in military trucks. The conditions in Juarez made the poverty in Chicago look like West Palm Beach.

The home where "the cartel" lived consisted of a piece of circular corrugated metal for walls with strips of metal welded and taped together for a ceiling. Cardboard boxes served as tables. The three families, with about 14 people, slept on the dirt floors in shifts due to the limited space. There was no running water or toilets. The following week, when the prosecutors watched our edited, narrated film, they agreed to reduce the charges. With further negotiation during the following month, the Hernandez brothers plead guilty to misdemeanors and were released with time served. Considering the State of Illinois was seeking life sentences for these guys, this was one huge victory. Greg and I referred to our day-in-the-life video as "Best Foreign Film Adapted for a Cartel."

We exited I-57 and drove into the town of Chester. Just before we made the final turn to get to the prison, I glanced out the window and noticed a great view of the Mississippi River. I asked Greg to pull over to take a look. Although the swiftly moving current between tree-lined banks was a beautiful sight, part of my motivation was to delay our arrival at Menard. It was not an easy place to be.

Greg steered the car onto a dirt shoulder, and, as we exited, we were greeted by the earthy smell of decaying leaves combined with the muddy, fishy scent. Looking into the murky waters, I mused how Gacy had disposed of four of his victims in the Des Plaines River 345 miles to the north. The map I had used on the trip down told me that the Des Plaines flows south to the Kankakee, forming the Illinois River, which is a tributary of the Mississippi whose mesmerizing currents were before me. The fate of these young men is forever connected to this waterway as ironically is the fate of John Wayne Gacy, whose final residence sits on a bluff overlooking it.

I was reminded of Mark Twain's great novel, *Huckleberry Finn*, and recalled my college professor telling us that the Mississippi symbolized freedom for Huck and Jim as they navigated the river on their little raft. Another irony. To me, this river will always signify confinement and the permanent surrender of freedom.

...

We arrived at Menard 15 minutes later. Pulling into the parking lot, I saw a sign I had somehow missed before: *No Alcohol or Firearms Allowed on Premises.* I laughed out loud. That is exactly what you need before entering this place.

Just because we were familiar with the drill conducted by the disdainful prison guards did not make it less humiliating and nerve-wracking. Nothing happened quickly in this building, and no one cared. It was well after 11:15 a.m. when we were finally admitted by buzzer into the condemned unit visitors' bullpen. Only about five guests were visiting, all appearing to be friends or family of the inmates. Gacy was in the same cinder block-walled cubicle as before. He appeared to be very agitated.

"Where the hell have youse guys been?" he demanded. His face was red, and his brow was visibly wet with sweat. "I told you to be here right at 9." He was not just agitated. He was hostile. So, this was the anger I had read about.

Greg and I looked at each other. Greg's expression seemed to say, "It's not my day to babysit. You control him." Greg also had a temper, and his first reaction to another person's anger was usually to return it.

"JW, we got a late start—which was my fault. We hit a bunch of traffic around Urbana. Then the fucking guards took their sweet time getting us in here …"

Gacy seated himself, angrily looking away.

When in doubt, tell him a joke, I thought.

"Okay. John Gacy had a doctor's appointment at 9 a.m. Dr. Smith walked in the examining room 30 minutes late. Dr. Smith said, 'Sorry John. I was stuck in traffic.' Gacy said, 'It's okay. I'm patient.'"

Gacy turned to me and without missing a beat said, "Greg Adamski went to his dentist appointment last week. He said, 'Doc, my teeth are yellow. What should I do?' The dentist said, 'Wear a brown tie.'"

We all laughed.

"Okay, John. What do you want to eat? I've got the quarters." Another diversion: Food. He wanted Fritos, two Hershey bars, and a Diet Coke. I beelined to the vending machine. After Gacy devoured his banquet of empty calories, we started our meeting as if the hissy fit had not occurred.

This time, our inmate had brought a large brown file that contained what he called his "Legal Stash." We talked about the appeals we were drafting. At this point, I talked a little bit about his trial, some 14 years earlier.

"So, JW. Your defense was insanity. Let's talk about the evidence the jury heard."

John told us he did not want to talk about trial. "It was a travesty of justice. Anyone who knows me knows I'm perfectly sane. I was working 20-hour days, building thousands of buildings, making lots of money, employing hundreds of people. All those bullshit shrinks didn't know nothin'. They said I had multiple personalities. Total crap."

He wanted to talk about all the media attention he was getting and who we were talking at the *Sun-Times* and Channel 9. He relished all attention he received, even though nothing the press said about the man was ever good. We turned to the topic of appeals. We had a slew of questions about the 14 -year chronology of appellate filings, and we wanted to get a list of all the lawyers who worked on his case so we could make sure we had a complete case file. Gacy had a fantastic memory, and I complimented him on it.

At that point, he sat back and said, "So, you grew up in Berwyn. Where exactly did you live?"

Quickly concluding that my client would never be out of jail to bother my mother who still lived in my childhood home, I gave him the cross streets. Although the suburb of Berwyn was not particularly close to Gacy's home in Norwood Park, he began to rattle off a detailed description of the elementary school I attended directly across the street from my house. He talked about the double-arched doors of the entrance, the "green-tinted soffit," and fenced-in grassed area where the flagpole stood.

Even though I had stared at the façade of this school at least 5,000 times in my life, I wasn't sure of some of these details. Was he bullshitting as he did constantly? Several weeks later, when visiting my mother, who had some stern words about the direction my career had taken, I confirmed all the details Gacy had recounted. I noted the building's soffit, made of copper, had developed a "green-tinted" patina over the years.

I tell you this because one of Gacy's many interesting personality traits was his exceptional visual memory. Even though he had been incarcerated for 14 years, he would often describe buildings and storefronts in the neighborhoods we mentioned.

On weekends, for fun, Greg and I would make what we called "Bullshit-Checking Trips" to the places Gacy had described.

On one occasion, he told me a story about some construction work he had performed in Cicero, Illinois, a Chicago suburb named after a Roman orator, but made famous by the business dealings of an Italian mobster, Al Capone. He talked about several buildings that lined Cermak Road, one of the main thoroughfares, describing the buildings' architecture and naming the stores that were in them.

When we later visited that neighborhood, we saw he was eerily accurate in his descriptions. On a subsequent prison trip, he noted that my hair had a different blonde tone, which he described as "honey-colored." Sure enough, a new hair stylist had suggested I subtly warm up my highlights. Nobody, including my husband, had noticed the difference.

Psychologists use the term "eidetic imagery" for people who can recall images in so much detail, clarity, and accuracy that it is as though the image is still being perceived. Typically found only in young children, the trait is virtually nonexistent in adults. It is thought that, as developmental changes occur, such as the acquisition of language skills, these types of abilities dissipate. It is also thought that eidetic imagery can impede the development of social skills.

When Gacy confessed his crimes to the police immediately after his arrest, he had an amazing recall of the visual details of the victims and the location of the buried bodies. Could this be a trait common to killers? Interestingly, Samuel Little, who far surpassed Gacy for his number of murders—93 spanning 19 states and 35 years—could accurately sketch lifelike depictions of his victims, some of whom he knew for only minutes and had murdered decades earlier.

...

Although Gacy's anger over our not being "on time" had subsided, it was still simmering beneath the surface when our lunch trays arrived. This time, I helped him carry them to our table.

According to Gacy, fellow inmates James Free and Hernando Williams had given up their meals for us. Coincidentally, ten months after Gacy's execution, these two men were executed on the same day, the first double execution in Illinois in 43 years.

Death penalty opponents contended Free, who was white, and Williams, who was black, were executed together to show that capital punishment was not discriminatory. Not interested in taking credit for equal opportunity executions, prison officials said it was because their appeals had ended at the same time. Both inmates had raped and killed women. Williams' crime was particularly brutal as he forced his 29-year-old victim into the trunk of his car and drove her around for 36 hours, raping her repeatedly, holding her there even as he attended a court hearing for a prior rape. Williams happened to be in the visitors' area that day as we seated ourselves. Gacy waved his hand gallantly nodding to him in thanks. Greg and I followed suit.

The meals smelled pretty good, but the visual left something to be desired. The entrée was chicken-fried something with sides of soggy fried potatoes, slimy carrots, a pasta salad with creamy dressing, and three slices of bread with fake butter. Again, two cartons of the orange drink. Just looking at this repast put my body into glycemic chaos. Gacy went right to town on his meal.

Greg grazed, politely eating a little bit of everything. Professing lack of hunger due to a late breakfast, I offered my meal to Gacy and he gladly accepted. During our power lunch, we continued to talk about the legal issues at hand. Gacy had a habit of bad-mouthing others and was in the process of denigrating the work of Greenlees and Keefe. (We later learned that he likewise badmouthed us to them.)

At some point, Greg testily told Gacy to stop and that his criticism was not productive. When the barbs continued, Greg reiterated that he was not going to hear this kind of talk. Gacy's earlier anger reappeared, and enraged, he grabbed a pint of the prison's disgusting orange drink and threw it across the table, smacking Greg in the face and splashing the syrupy beverage all over his tie. Greg, who was an imposing figure at 6'1," 250 pounds, was not one to back down from any man, even one with only a few months left to live.

Greg flew to his feet and pushed the table into Gacy's chest. He almost fell back in his chair but managed to scramble to his feet. The two of them stood up and started yelling at each other. When I lunged to insert myself between them, from the corner of my eye, I saw the other inmates (all killers, mind you) begin to move toward our cubicle. Notably absent were any prison guards.

Realizing that a death row rumble was about to occur, I shouted, "Stop it or you're both going to end up in jail!"

Gacy looked at me with a blank face and then started chuckling. Then I starting laughing. And then Greg did too. The altercation was over. I would realize that Gacy's mood changes were mercurial and extreme. It seemed he feigned anger and then calmed down at will, making it hard to tell what was real emotion and what was not.

As we sat down, I tried to soothe the two male egos. "Someone needs to apologize here," I said maternally.

"Sorry, Greg. Got a lot on my mind," Gacy's demeanor a study in simulated regret.

"Apology accepted," said Greg still trying to dab the orange liquid off his silk tie. *Silk is so unforgiving*, I thought.

Gacy, always the joker cracked, "Your dentist *told* you, Greg: You should have worn a brown tie."

I just had to: "And orange you glad you didn't!"

Enjoying our death row comedy, we finished our lunch on a high note with Greg graciously giving Gacy his orange beverage to replace the liquid that was still dripping down his tie.

It was on this visit we tried to push Gacy to discuss the

crimes. Even though he reportedly confessed willingly to all the crimes following his arrest in a surreal and lengthy police interview, he thereafter began denying this confession and maintaining his complete innocence. His position with us was he did not kill any of the victims on his property or in the river except for the first victim—"The Greyhound Bus Station Boy."

Just after the New Year in 1972, 16-year-old Timothy McVoy made the life-ending mistake of stopping for a layover at the Chicago Greyhound bus station just blocks away from where Gacy was employed at Bruno's Restaurant. Bruno's was an old-fashioned supper club that had a strange mix of clientele. There were local athletes and television personalities as well as cops and politicians and members of Chicago's Outfit. Gacy would work all night as a cook and return to his house in the early hours of the morning.

Gacy told us that he had picked up the boy and taken him to his home where they had consensual sex. Afterward, the boy, "a sleazy, greedy hustler," came at him with a knife, and in self-defense, Gacy "stabbed the fucker in his chest four or five times." He complained that the boy was "going to get blood all over my rug." That was the only killing for which he was responsible. As to the rest, he had no idea "who those bodies were."

Greg was not in a patient mood, his face and neck still sticky with orange beverage. "C'mon John. If you're innocent, why were there all those bodies under your house?"

He then pulled from his file a black notebook that looked like something I used in seventh grade. It was about six inches thick and had multicolored reference tabs. He was handling it like it was precious cargo. Almost reluctantly, he set it down on the table and pushed it toward us as if to say, "This explains everything."

A bold label on the notebook's front cover read: *The Body Book*. Intrigued, I picked it up and began flipping through it. The pages contained a "scrapbook" of Gacy's victims, separated by colored tabs with a corresponding index. For each young man, there was a dossier of personal facts: Date of birth, age at the time of disappearance, hospital of birth, schools attended, names of parents and siblings. For some of the victims, there were family photographs, news clippings of school sports and other achievements, yearbook entries, and pictures of childhood homes. Most troubling were the newspaper stories announcing their disappearances. Chills went down my spine.

"What in the hell is this, John?" I asked. "Who put this together and why?"

He proceeded to explain that he had paid a young man by the name of Randy White to compile these materials. The reason? He wanted to figure out how these bodies came to be buried under his house—which would help him find the "true" killer.

Greg and I looked at each other with raised eyebrows. There was no question in my mind that the scrapbook was an assemblage of serial killer souvenirs, Gacy's way of holding onto his victims and remembering the crimes. Serial killers are known to take trophies from their victims. Keeping some memento, a lock of hair, jewelry, or newspaper clipping of the crime helps prolong, even nourish, their fantasy of the crime.

When his home was searched, police found these types of objects that belonged to his victims—school rings, driver's licenses, combs, and other pocket items. As it turned out, his souvenir collection helped him earn a permanent vacation to this correctional center. And looking back, I now understand that by keeping the bodies under his house rather than disposing of them elsewhere, he was simply keeping his victims close.

"John, I don't understand the title. *The Body Book.* These are boys and men, not bodies."

His answer was unsettling and ignored my question. "Yes, but where were their parents when these kids were running away or hanging out at bus stations?" He was telling me these human beings deserved to die. Calling them "bodies" was his way of dehumanizing them to justify the taking of their lives. I never saw that book again, and no one seems to know what happened to it.

We left right at 3 p.m. when visiting hours ended. We did not consider leaving a minute earlier given our unforgivable late arrival. We did not need another food fight. We were weary and in Greg's case, sticky. Spending time in a prison is like dog years. Every hour seems like seven. We listlessly made our way out of the labyrinth-like passageways with the surly guards begrudgingly opening doors and slamming them behind us in no hurry to see us on our way.

Exiting the prison into the crisp air, we felt relief. We plopped in the car and with the scent of orange drink wafting through the car like a bad air freshener, I fell into a deep sleep.

After what must have been two hours into my nap, I suddenly awoke from a pleasant dream to Greg's shouting, "No! No!"

I looked at his terrified face and then ahead into the darkness. Loping across our path from the left was a massive animal. I screamed for Greg to stop as he swerved to the right and slammed on the brakes. Our car skidded, the screeching rising above our shouts. The world clicked to slow motion. A buck stood directly in our path, its antlered head turned to look directly at us, eyes glowing unnaturally, dilated with fear.

I turned my head to look away as if my flinching would somehow allow us to avoid contact. I heard a loud and sickening thud. Looking back to the road, I saw the buck had been propelled ahead of us, on its side, legs flailing helplessly, all prior dignity gone. Our car had come to a stop. The injured creature was facing toward his aborted destination on the other side of the road, one of his obsidian eyes locked on ours. He shuddered, let out a loud guttural groan, and then surprisingly struggled to his feet, instincts and adrenaline taking control of his body. Shaking his majestic head, he bravely dragged his broken body off the asphalt into the serenity of the thick woods.

Saddened and frightened, I exited the car. Greg was already out assessing the damage. Expensive but drivable, the diagnosis.

We got back in our seats shaken to the core. I kept thinking of the horrible noise of the deer hitting our bumper and the certain damage done to its internal organs. What would become of that magnificent creature? Did he find a place among the trees to wait for death to arrive, alone in the privacy of nature? Had he already succumbed to his fate? Tears came to my eyes. Could we have avoided this tragedy? Or was this animal's destiny predetermined once it set foot on this rural road? I got little comfort from the bleak realization that I probably never had any control over the animal's life or death. The fact was this animal would soon be dead.

The lesson is that all living things have a genetically-embedded force driving them to deny death no matter their knowledge of this fait accompli.

15.

HAVE YOURSELF A MERRY LITTLE CHRISTMAS

After our November 1993 prison visit, we did not plan to see Gacy until the new year. We were busy in Chicago crafting our legal missives that would be launched closer to the scheduled execution date. Normally, litigation slows during the holidays as litigants tend to put down their boxing gloves to engage in alternatively stressful endeavors such as Christmas shopping, dealing with children at home, and attending family gatherings. Come January, they welcome their litigation disputes back into their daily lives.

In the 1990s, holiday parties were at their peak. It would not be unusual to be invited to several gatherings every week from the end of November until Christmas, sometimes multiple parties on the same evening. Some of them were held at fancy hotels and restaurants, some in decorated office suites, but all of them offered plenty of heavy appetizers and strong drinks.

In 1993, Greg and I received an inordinate number of invites, which I truly believed was due to our newfound celebrity as "lawyers for a serial killer." Lawyers in the Chicago legal community knew we were representing him and were fascinated by it. With festive cocktail in hand, everyone wanted to know how we got involved, what our litigation strategy was, and most importantly, what was he really like?

There are some people for whom holidays are a great

source of joy, harkening back to their childhoods filled with the magic of family, friends, and celebration. I have never been one of those people. I don't hate the holidays, but they cause me to become melancholy and subdued, and to feel as if I am missing out on something that others are experiencing.

I also feel a sense of obligation to do things I don't want to do. This bah humbug attitude is out of character for me because I'm usually an upbeat and positive person. I know myself well enough to understand that my darkness will dissipate shortly after the ball drops in Times Square and the holidays are behind me.

Because Gacy and I were talking on almost a daily basis throughout the holiday season, I could sense that he, too, was becoming morose and a bit less spirited. According to the psychiatrists who examined Gacy, Christmas was a significant time in his development as a killer. While he was in prison in Iowa in his first run-in with the legal system, his father died on Christmas Day 1969. His request to attend the funeral was denied. Despite the terrible relationship he had with his father, Gacy still longed for his love and respect—something he never had. He took his father's death particularly hard, believing it was caused by the shame he felt having his only son incarcerated for homosexual crimes.

Throughout his childhood, Gacy's father had accused him of being gay, which was finally proven true by the charges and guilty verdict in Iowa. Gacy gave me conflicting accounts about his father. He said that his father exhibited frequent "Jekyll and Hyde" personality changes precipitated by daily drinking binges in the family basement, evolving into beatings of the entire family with a razor strop.

Although he showed affection for his father, the senior Gacy always found fault with him, and Gacy felt he could never be as "perfect" as his father demanded. Other sources indicate Gacy was disinterested in the traditionally male activities enjoyed by his father such as sports, fishing, hunting, and camping, and would rather spend time with his mother gardening and cooking.

Despite these stories, he would often defend his father.

"My dad was not the alcoholic monster the media made him out to be. I never said I hated him."

"But John, beating you and your mother and making fun of you was wrong," I'd counter.

"My father taught me values and morals."

"Oh, really. What values and morals, John?"

Apropos of nothing, Gacy posited, "The way to remember my dad is to not be like him. That's how you get back at the son of a bitch."

This waffling view of his father was seen by psychiatrists as lack of "integration." Most of us have a code, a rudder that makes what we say consistent for the most part. So, when you get to know someone, you can generally predict what they think and how they will react. Gacy had no such compass. He said the first thing that came to his mind or what he thought someone wanted to hear.

On one hand, he was prim, proper, and Catholic and on the other immoral, vulgar, and profane. He was rigid and lacking in affect, and then he was hilarious and seemingly compassionate. He was smart but spouted ignorant thoughts and opinions. He was a homosexual and open-minded, but the next minute he was critical of gays and minorities. He had disdain for his fellow inmates based upon their crimes, and yet he was guilty of the most heinous of them.

"John, are you like your dad or not? You say you don't like gay men, but you are one. Some of the boys under your house you claim were gay. I'm confused."

He blurted, "Why would I want to kill these boys? I am not their father." Was he saying he thought his father wanted to kill him? Or did he put himself in his father's shoes when he killed boys that reminded him of himself? According to forensic psychiatrist Dr. Richard Rappaport, who had spent 65 hours examining Gacy in preparation for his trial and the insanity defense, the trauma of his father's abuse was central to his mental and emotional dysfunction. "The relationship that went on between the two of them was the forerunner for the relationship he had with his victims," Rappaport's report stated. The burial of bodies in the crawlspace beneath his home was related to the location in his childhood home where he'd suffered physical abuse as a child at the hands of his father.

The handcuffing of his victims was also telling.

According to Rappaport, "He was putting on a scenario that reenacted the way he felt as a child. He was essentially getting them to play his role of being helpless ... while he played the role of the father. And he'd punish them for begging him, and for looking like cowards—whatever he felt about his own inadequacies, he put on them."

The more I heard Gacy talk about his father, the more strongly I believe it was his father who was the catalyst for creating the monster in him. The old saying "Hurt people hurt people" is very true, having dealt with both the hurt and the hurters.

As much as Gacy gave lip service to not wanting to be his father, in some ways, that is exactly who he became. And worse.

...

As a typical sociopath who tried to act as the normal world thought he should, Gacy did what was expected during the holidays. He sent Christmas cards to me, Greg, and our office staff. The cards were religious in nature and contained what appeared to be heartfelt appreciation for the work we were doing.

Although I had long ago given up the seasonable tradition of sending out Christmas cards, I felt the urge to brave the cold Chicago weather and walk the several windy blocks to Papyrus to buy the only card I would buy that year.

As I walked in, the clerk asked if she could help me. I would have loved to say, "Death row inmate section, please?"

I gave her the "I'm okay" wave and began culling through the holiday cards eliminating any that included a New Year's wish. (Why give Gacy false hope?)

After about five minutes, I scored big. On the front: A

drunk-looking Santa Claus with a clown's nose. Inside was printed: "Santa Claus is Coming to Clown."

"Dear JW," I wrote, "If I can get in the Christmas spirit, so the hell can you. Merry Christmas!"

16.

THE COURT OF PUBLIC OPINION

After the holidays were over, things got back to their normal pace for a short time: the calm before the storm. Media outlets were demanding our attention, not just in Chicago but throughout the country and internationally. I want to talk about publicity and the power of the media because it is a big part of how representing Gacy changed my life during the seven months I represented him and how it continues to change it to this day.

I took on the lead as Gacy's spokesperson because I knew that the existence of capital punishment was dependent upon public opinion. The history of the death penalty shows that public opinion dictates whether a country or state utilizes death as a punishment. Over the years, public opinion has risen in favor of it and then has ebbed. For instance, after World War II and the Nazi atrocities, people in the United States were not in favor of executing inmates. In the 1980s, the approval rating for it increased. Right now, our socially aware younger generation has increasingly disfavored the punishment. As with any emotional issue, education is the way to change people's minds, not arrogant and erudite rantings. I believed if I could alter even one person's opinion, I was doing something for the cause. The media element was crucial to get the word out.

The question now was how to approach the press to get

the job done properly. Given Gacy's horrible reputation, I knew this was going to be a real challenge. I did not believe "all publicity is good publicity." If this were to be my 15 minutes of influence, it had better reflect well on the cause and myself. Greg and I decided to seek out professional advice about how to present ourselves before the media so as not to look like idiots or appear as though we were trying to excuse Gacy's horrific acts.

We knew of a public relations firm in Chicago that had helped a local personal injury attorney procure media appearances to talk about plane crashes, class actions, and other large-dollar legal cases. The lawyer in question was very attractive and glib, but lacked experience in the courtroom. Much to the amazement of Chicago's legal community, the PR skills the lawyer acquired allowed her to score lucrative cases that were settled and tried by competent lawyers who worked for her, netting her millions of dollars. Last I heard, she was selling her $27 million mansion and upgrading. I am not praising or criticizing this business model, but if this attorney's success could be at least partially attributed to this PR firm's advice, they were the ones I wanted helping me.

I made an appointment for a consult, and two days later, the tall, handsome male and female team came to our office. The woman, I learned later, had been a runner-up in the Miss America Pageant and still carried herself as if there were a crown on her head. Who better to teach me about poise, appearance, and answering questions with a smile on my face? At least I didn't have to do it wearing a bathing suit.

The PR team spent the next two hours giving me the advice I needed—how to dress, wear makeup, and style my hair; how to talk in sound bites if it were television, and how to answer in 30-second segments if it were radio. For each interview, I would come equipped with five points, and no matter what I was asked, I would spit them out in response. If they were well thought out and pithy, the media would use them. I also learned to give individual interviews, if possible, rather than press conferences. It was easier for a reporter to smear you when multiple reporters were present.

If you spoke to reporters one-on-one and helped them do their job by providing copies of the briefs, summarizing the arguments, and explaining the legal maneuverings, they would usually respect you and were much less likely to make you look foolish or make a negative association because of who your client was. It was also important to let reporters know that if they screwed you over, you would decline all further interviews with them. They might think the "making you look bad" story sells, but there is no story if the lawyers refuse to talk.

I immediately followed the advice I was given. I bought the right makeup, selected the specific solid-colored clothing, and practiced my pitch on a recording device until I eliminated the "you knows" and "ums" as best I could. I did my homework, compiled thick files of data, and memorized catchy phrases and examples to illustrate my arguments. Although I struggled at first, I became fairly adept at handling the media inquiries whether they occurred in prescheduled interviews, while I was walking down the street, or on the steps of my home. I learned to dress the part no matter where I was or what time it was. When the case heated up, there was nowhere we could go to avoid public attention over one of the most sensational executions in the country's history.

It is difficult to describe the onslaught of media attention. It started in earnest in February and March when we began filing lawsuits, petitions, and appeals. It was overwhelming and constant. Some days, I would spend a full eight hours giving interviews on radio, television, to newspapers and magazines, explaining our position and advocating against the death penalty.

My secretary spent the majority of her day returning phone calls, scheduling interviews, faxing briefs to reporters, and advising them of upcoming court dates. The reporters largely focused on the salacious facts about Gacy and begged us to help them get permission to bring cameras into the prison for interviews, something over which we had no control.

Several lawsuits were filed by national news outlets to

force Menard to allow such interviews. All were denied for safety concerns. I am still not sure who was in danger: the reporters or Gacy.

One beautiful, raven-haired television reporter from Rome had imbedded herself in Chicago for three months before the execution and had taken to hanging around our law office, bringing us bottles of red wine she had found in the local liquor stores and complaining with her heavy accent that she had packed the wrong clothes for "this city that freezes."

Between elegant hair tosses, the signora expressed her distress that our great country was still using "this barbaric practice." Focusing her female wiles on Greg, she told him in no uncertain terms and with a cross of her stocking-covered legs that "she would do anything to interview Mr. Gacy," including becoming "friendly" with the prison guards. Either she had never met the guards at Menard or I underestimated her dedication.

On a Friday in May, my picture was on the front page of all three Chicago newspapers. Within 24 hours, I was interviewed by every national television news network and all four local stations. A friend who was honeymooning in a treehouse in a Costa Rican rainforest called to tell me she turned on her television to see my face on CNN. Greg's relatives in Poland phoned to say they saw our interview dubbed in Polish on their local network. Whether we were eating breakfast at 7 a.m. on the west side of Chicago, going for a haircut in the Gold Coast, or working out at a gym in the suburbs, the reporters would be there pushing their way in to get access to us. On one occasion, a reporter had given our car park valet a $20 bill to allow him to trespass on the lot to wait by our car with his cameraman. Not figuring we would leave our office as late as 9 p.m., the guys waited there for four hours in the cold.

I was naïve to think the public would respond to our representation neutrally. I somehow believed people would understand everyone deserves a defense, especially in a capital case and that Gacy, who was almost guaranteed his date with death, was entitled to a lawyer. It is part of our justice system. I thought if I acknowledged Gacy's crimes, acted respectfully, and avoided lecturing about the death penalty in a pedantic way, people would at least not hate me. That largely did not happen. And rage-filled people are more vocal. My mother used to say, "Life is not a popularity contest," and although I have my doubts about this adage, if there was one in Spring 1994, I would have come in dead last.

Where do I start about the negative fallout? I received thousands of calls, letters, packages, and personal confrontations. The normal letters asked, "How could you lend yourself to this?" and, "Don't you have respect for the victims' families?"

Among my other detractors: childhood friends, neighbors, a high school teacher who "before this, thought I would make our school proud," a Christian minister, an old boyfriend, and several "innocent" prisoners in other states who were angry I was working for free for a guilty person and not them.

When I attended a fundraiser for the Illinois State Treasurer, Judy Baar Topinka, a woman who had been my mentor and friend for 20 years, she almost tripped and fell trying to escape a photographer who was getting ready to take a picture of us greeting each other. Judy, an avid animal rights activist, later said to me, "Karen, you have your job to do, but sometimes you have to put the dangerous dog down."

One of the local law schools held a large anti-death penalty symposium in conjunction with Sister Helen Prejean and her organization. Prejean is the author of the book *Dead Man Walking*, which was made into a movie with Sean Penn and Susan Sarandon, who won the Oscar for her portrayal of Prejean.

When my assistant called to get tickets, she was put on hold and then disconnected. Later, one of the organizers called to tell us it was best for the Gacy's lawyers not to be involved in the event as it would only serve to work against the cause.

I received many disturbing letters of a sexual nature. One tenacious correspondent sent me at least 30 letters over the years, some well after Gacy was executed. His letters (I picture him as male, middle-aged, and living in his mother's basement) always included a creative collage made up of pictures of men's and women's body parts and genitals, Hollywood celebrity photos, pictures of Mount Rushmore, texts from the Bible, and wrappers from feminine hygiene products. He would laboriously arrange them on notebook paper with his heavy jagged printing berating me for my "sick and twisted" obsession with Gacy. His letters would almost always end with a request for my autograph or something from my lingerie drawer.

There were numerous threats, most of them directed toward me rather than the other three lawyers on the team. I reported several seemingly serious ones to the police who were largely unconcerned and largely unsympathetic. Despite my entreaties, no officer would take a report. Until we got the bomb threat.

Two typed messages were delivered to our lobby desk and at the building management office demanding our eviction. The note stated that lawyers who represent John Gacy should meet with the same fate as their client. The notes warned that bombs had been placed in strategic places in the building and underneath the building in the pedway leading to the Chicago Transit "El" stops. Six floors of professionals were evacuated while the bomb squad did a public safety sweep throughout the building and underground. I still see one of the tenants from the floor beneath me who kids me about the time we almost got "bombed" together.

I received one disturbing letter from a prisoner in Alabama who was serving two life sentences for raping, murdering, and burying two young women near Huntsville. After explaining that he saw me on television and thought I was a "hot chick," he casually segued into confessing to killing over 40 women and burying them within two miles of the other victims. The way he described it, you could not go for a walk in Madison County, Alabama without stepping over some of his subterranean handiwork. He gave me specific locations of several of his victims in the manner of a funeral director, proud of his expert burial techniques. He proposed I become his lawyer to cut a deal with the county prosecutor: He would confess to all these crimes and take authorities to the locations of the remains. In exchange for such civic-minded honesty, he would be released from prison. I struggled not to turn over this letter to authorities, but attorney-client confidentiality concerns prevented me from doing so. For years after, I checked this guy's name in the Alabama inmate search. I'm not sure if I wanted to see if he had ever been convicted of those additional crimes or to make certain he was still safely behind bars.

In late January, I was sitting in Greg's office discussing a strategy for filing a federal appeals brief. Our secretary announced a call from one of our favorite clients. I will call him David French. David was the owner of one of the nation's largest medical filing system companies, which provided labels and folders for physicians to organize patient information. There is no such business today because this data is all digital. David had hired us to sue a former salesman who was violating his non-compete clause, stealing customers, costing David thousands of dollars in lost revenue. David's call was put through to Greg's speaker phone.

"Greg, Karen. I have something serious to discuss with you.

"Okay," said Greg. "Shoot."

"My wife just told me she saw you guys on television, and you're representing John Gacy. Is that true?"

"Yes," Greg and I answered in unison.

"Okay. Is Gacy's file in the same file cabinet as mine?"

We looked at each other, puzzled. "Yes."

"Okay. And is his file next to mine?" David always thought in terms of alphabetic filing cabinet position due to the nature of his business.

Greg scanned our client list which sat on his desk. "Yes, David. Gacy comes after French."

Pause. "I love you guys and you've been great to me. But I cannot have lawyers who are representing a God damn monster. And I can't even sleep at night thinking his file is touching mine. I've got to hire new counsel."

Greg picked up the phone to talk to David. I walked out, thinking, *really*?

Despite Greg's well-known persuasive abilities, he lost

this battle. David fired us and we respectfully withdrew as his lawyers and transitioned the file to new counsel. Not only did we lose what could have amounted to $150,000 in fees for his injunction case, we also lost an ongoing client and friendship. File that one under "The Gacy Effect."

The fallout went on and on. When I appeared in court on other cases, judges made sarcastic and derogatory comments to me. One judge held my case to the end of the two-hour call even though the docket had me listed as first in line. When my case was finally called, the judge asked me to come into chambers. Without even asking me to sit, he turned to me and heatedly told me that he didn't appreciate the way my representation of Gacy was reflecting on the legal community.

He told me, "This is making us all look bad," and "Let the man, die for God's sake." Judges decide your clients' fates and may be on the bench for decades, so you cannot fight or be disrespectful. I just stood there and took the tongue-lashing. For years before the judge finally retired, I tried as best I could to avoid appearing in front of him because every time he set eyes on me, he looked like he had just eaten a dish full of maggots. If anyone should have understood a defendant's right to counsel, it should have been a judge. He was not the only person whose rules changed when it came to Gacy.

On the home front, strangers constantly drove past our house and several threw things on our lawn. One morning, there were two gallons of what appeared to be ketchup on my front stairs. It was either a symbol signifying the spillage of blood by some antagonist or a Heinz delivery gone awry.

In 1994, guns of any type were greatly disfavored by residents of liberal Oak Park and handguns were illegal there, the U.S. Supreme Court having yet to issue its ruling announcing that everyone had a Second Amendment right to a gun. Our neighbor, a father of five and former volunteer for the Peace Corps, came to our house one spring day to advise us we were creating a "neighborhood nuisance" by representing a child killer. Days later, he purchased a rifle, which he kept by his door. His window posted a sticker reading, "The Owner of This Property is Armed and There is Nothing Here Worth Dying For." So much for my peace-loving neighbor.

And last but not least, after work one evening, Greg, his son, and I stopped into a local Italian joint for some pasta primavera. Three young men at a high-top bar table began gesturing to us, clearly agitated. They recognized us from an interview we had given earlier that day and which had just aired on the bar television. The men became profane and loud. The manager came over, spoke to them, and then politely asked us to leave. "I was more in the mood for Greek anyway," I told him with a smile.

Note: While I was doing a final proofread of this chapter, I clicked on my emails, and there in my inbox was a lengthy hate email from a woman who had seen me on a Gacy documentary that had recently been aired. You can tell a person's anger level by the number of font changes, exclamation points, F-bombs, and capital letters. This one had three font changes, 16 exclamation points, five F-bombs, and the whole thing was in caps.

She criticized me for loving pedophiles, bad makeup application, vacant eyes, stupidity, infertility, and a "shriveled soul."

Remember, it had been almost three decades since Gacy died and she was still angry at me for representing him. I then did what I routinely do when I receive such a missive: I friended her (Claudia) on Facebook and then Googled her to calculate how far away the threat was. This hater appeared to live in England, so I figured she would at least HAVE SOME F*****ING COOLING OFF TIME BEFORE SHE GOT TO ME!!!!!!!!!!!!!!!!!

17.

THE THRILL OF VICTORY

In February, I received a call from a law professor at the University of Illinois who taught me criminal law during my first semester when I was just 21 years old. After catching up on each other's lives and exchanging law school gossip, he told me he had some creative ideas about how to attack the death penalty.

With a Ph.D. and honors law degree from Harvard University, Francis Boyle was someone with whom you easily could disagree but rarely outthink. He was left of left, a true academic, and a true believer. Over the years, he represented the government of Bosnia, assisted in the indictment of Slobodan Milosević for genocide, advocated for Native American tribes, and drafted the Biological Weapons Anti-Terrorism Act of 1989 signed into law by President George H.W. Bush, the only time Boyle had ever sided with a Republican. He also represented the Nation of Hawaii in its efforts to secede from the United States, an issue I debated with him seeing as I love to vacation in Maui and would have resented having to leave our country to do so.

Criminal law had been my favorite law school subject. We learned that today's laws date back to Hammurabi's Code devised in the 1700s B.C. by a Babylonian King, a time when cruel and unusual had a whole different meaning. We had provocative discussions on issues of right and wrong, what is punishable and what is forgivable, what can negate a person's intent to commit a crime, and what can mitigate culpability.

We studied the differences between first- and second-degree murder, sex crimes, defenses of intoxication and mistake, what it means to conspire, and to aid and abet. Little did I know that my favorite lecture—The Insanity Defense—would come in handy representing the highest-profile client of my career. Moral of the story: Pay attention in school. You never know when a subject will be important. I still haven't used geometry, but the insanity defense, I have.

Professor Boyle and I briefly discussed over the telephone whether Gacy's insanity defense could have been successful. Gacy's position at trial, some 14 years before my involvement, was that he was insane at the time of the crimes and therefore was not guilty by reason of insanity. Many people ask me, "How can a person like Gacy *not* be insane —killing and burying kids under his house?"

I once asked Gacy about his trial lawyer's decision to lodge the insanity defense.

He became agitated and complained, "The insanity defense is bullshit."

"Why, John?"

"Well, it doesn't work. Take Jeffrey Dahmer. Now, I don't know Jeff, but here's a guy who wakes up in the morning. His body is encrusted with blood and there's a severed head in his fridge, and his first thought is: Hey, I wanna fuck that torso next to me! If *that* guy isn't insane, I'd hate to run into the guy who is!" Gacy could not have said it better. The insanity defense is not very useful to killers. As Professor Boyle taught me, here's why.

Originating in 1843 in Great Britain, the defense was first used by a man named M'Naughten who shot and killed the secretary to the Prime Minister believing he was the Prime Minister. He claimed the Tories were conspiring against him. At trial, M'Naughten's counsel put forth a defense of insanity, offering expert testimony and other evidence in support. The jury was instructed that all defendants are presumed to be sane unless they can prove that, at the time the criminal act was committed, the defendant's state of mind caused him to (1) not know what he was doing when he committed said act, or (2) that he knew what he was doing but did not know that it was wrong. Under what is now called "The M'Naughten Test," the jury returned a verdict of not guilty "by reason of insanity" and M'Naughten spent the rest of his life in a mental institution.

Over the years, half of the states still use this test and other states have implemented different variations. Under Illinois law, "a defendant may be excused from criminal conduct if he can prove by clear and convincing evidence that he suffered a mental disease or defect that caused him to lack substantial capacity to appreciate the criminality of his conduct or conform his conduct to the requirements of law." Therefore, it's not enough for an accused to have a mental disease; that disease must have caused him to lack an understanding that his acts were criminal.

And therein lies the difficulty with a murderer using the insanity defense: Most killers commit the crimes in secret, flee from the crime, hide the evidence, don't admit to doing them, and otherwise act so as not to get caught. These actions demonstrate the criminal knows murder is a crime and that getting caught would mean punishment. Therefore, if Gacy were to prove that he was mentally defective—(seems like a slam-dunk)—he would still have a heck of a time proving he didn't know that kidnapping, raping, and murdering young men is wrong when he took every possible step to cover up the crimes.

Although you hear a lot about the insanity defense, it is very rarely invoked and even more rarely successful. A notorious example of the insanity defense working is the case of John Hinckley Jr. who shot President Ronald Reagan, injured a police officer, a Secret Service agent, and Reagan's press secretary, James Brady. At trial, Hinckley claimed he had become obsessed with actress Jodie Foster, specifically with her role as a child prostitute in the 1976 Martin Scorsese film *Taxi Driver*. Instead of dazzling Foster with his personality, or at least one of them, Hinckley decided the best way to impress her would be to kill the President of the United States. The experts diagnosed him with schizophrenia and major depression, which caused delusions and breaks in reality. Hinckley was institutionalized for 35 years and finally released in 2016.

Gacy was examined and tested for over 300 hours by numerous experts who testified extensively at trial. The complicated diagnoses would require substantial training to fully understand. Most of the doctors concluded that he had an antisocial personality disorder, borderline personality, and paranoid schizophrenia. Antisocial personality disorder, also known as "psychopathy," is characterized by a total disregard for the feelings of others. They lie, act out violently, break the law, and show no remorse. Borderline personalities behave impulsively, and have intense mood swings, feelings of low self-worth, and problems in interpersonal relationships. Many borderlines have been sexually abused at an early age. Schizophrenics list symptoms ranging from hallucinations and delusions to emotional flatness.

In Gacy's case, some doctors believed that his schizophrenia caused psychotic episodes that resulted in him taking actions over which he had no control. The doctors consistently found that his deviance came from environmental factors: the abuse and emotional neglect of his father, confusion, and repression of his sexuality, and sexual molestation as a child. As one psychiatrist succinctly put it: During the murders, he was killing the parts of himself he didn't like. However, from a legal standpoint, it didn't matter. He still knew what he was doing was wrong.

The jury rejected the insanity defense and found Gacy guilty in under two hours, one hour shorter than the average baseball game. Not only is the defense a hard one to prove, but most jurors who worry about the future dangerousness of an accused don't care if he's evil or crazy; they just want to make sure he is locked up. A mental institution is often viewed as a less permanent place of detention than a prison. The decision by the trial lawyers to argue insanity was not a difficult one. Despite the poor chances of it succeeding, there was no other choice. Actual innocence or self-defense would have been laughable.

After expressing skepticism that an appellate attack on the use of the insanity defense would be successful, Professor Boyle said he had an idea. Given that countries outside the United States overwhelmingly disfavored capital punishment, why not use international law to overturn the death sentence? He suggested that we meet in person at O'Hare Airport in a few days when he had a layover before an international flight. I readily agreed. The more brains on this case, the better. Creativity was welcomed at this stage of the game.

In the late afternoon of the following Tuesday, I took a cab to O'Hare Airport. Traffic was unusually congested, taking an hour and ten minutes to finally reach the terminal. We agreed to meet near the United Airlines international ticket counter. After five minutes of dodging distracted passengers and luggage carts, I spotted Professor Boyle standing a few yards away, a small carry-on in hand and a navy blue wool dress coat over his shoulder. Other than a few more strands of "wisdom highlights" woven into his tousled strands, he looked the same: thin, wiry, and constantly in motion.

Smiling at each other, we awkwardly hugged, unsure how to greet each other now that 11 years had passed since we were professor and student. We found a relatively quiet bench and sat down. Boyle, ever the professor, lectured me patiently on the international laws that governed how the death penalty was implemented. In particular, the Inter-American Commission on Human Rights, headquartered in Washington, D.C., was formed to promote and protect human rights in the American hemisphere. The core of the organization's tenets is the *American Declaration of the Rights and Duties of Man* and the *American Convention on Human Rights*. Even though these proclamations do not have treaty status, they are supposed to be binding obligations for the member states.

"Okay," I said, "How does this organization have the authority to stop an execution? I am certain these organizations will find that much of what goes on in Illinois executions to be objectionable, but how will a ruling by this body have any teeth when it comes to stopping the execution?"

Professor Boyle cocked his head and said with a grin, "Why don't we just see what happens?"

As an academic, Boyle had an interest in making his point and setting a precedent. I had the same interest, but I had a more immediate goal of preventing a human life from being extinguished. Despite our slightly divergent interests, if Boyle led the way, I was willing to help write this petition and dive into the waters of international law. Professor Boyle went on his merry way, off to save the world from injustice, and I returned to the office with yet another task on my plate to try to save Gacy's life.

Working with someone as smart as Francis Boyle was a treat. He was an aggressive advocate and knew how to turn his academic understanding of an issue into a compelling argument. Most kids entering law school think that the practice of law is all Perry Mason court moments, "gotcha" cross-examination, and dramatic closing arguments. Only three or four percent of all cases go to trial, so much of your work is "pretrial," which depends upon the written word. The motions, petitions, and briefs are largely argued on paper with the courts declining to hear oral argument. So, your writing must be clear, concise, and entertaining; it must convey the importance of the argument and the righteousness of your request.

While occasionally good writers are born, you become good at writing by spending lots of time doing it, allowing a better writer to edit your work, and then continuing to edit it again and again, keeping in mind there is almost always a better way to say something. The relief from this painful process comes when a judge understands your argument, sides with your view of the issue, and rules in your client's favor.

Boyle and I worked together writing the argument, with Boyle taking the lead. In the end, the petition read beautifully. We argued that the lethal injection machine invented by Fred Leuchter, an admitted and proud Holocaust denier, had malfunctioned repeatedly when used in the past. Therefore, that method of execution constituted torture under international law. We also argued that, because Leuchter based his invention's mechanics on research done by the Nazis on Jews during World War II, this too violated international law as the use of such research was strictly prohibited by treaty for obvious reasons. We submitted the petition via fax machine and hoped for the best.

We didn't have to wait long because within 48 hours, the Inter-American Commission issued its brief but decisive edict: If used, Illinois' lethal injection machine would violate international law. Given the lack of positive results thus far in representing Gacy, I was stunned. Now what? The edict was an anomaly. This kind of foray into international law was not done regularly so there was no precedent for how such a ruling could or would be used by the State of Illinois.

As it turns out, we did not have long to celebrate our win. Just days after submitting the Commission's ruling to our governor, his office announced that the State of Illinois would not be bound by the tribunal's ruling or at least when it came to John Wayne Gacy. Our win in the international forum turned into another lost battle on the way to losing the war. Sportscaster Vin Scully was wise when he said, "Losing hurts worse than winning feels good." The thrill of victory is short, but the agony of defeat lasts a lifetime.

18.

THE NIGHT BEFORE THE EXECUTION
May 9, 1994
11:42 p.m.

Gacy and his entourage have arrived at the place where he will die. The room where he will take his last breath. The gurney sits in the center of the chamber, with its leather straps dangling off the bright white sheets, proudly laundered and starched by the prison laundry team. Gacy does not look at it, pretending this is not happening. He is good at pretending, lying to himself and others his whole life, denying responsibility for what he did and who he was. Delusion certainly comes in handy now.

His caretakers politely help hoist him up on the gurney. His blue shirt is neatly pressed. His prison pants bunch up around his knees as he is slid down to the middle of the death bed. His face is devoid of expression, his slate-blue eyes flat and lifeless, all reflecting his lack of human emotion, a sociopath to the end. He's a man capable of killing a boy after torturing him for hours and then eating a ham sandwich over his still-warm body.

Gacy briefly looks up over his shoulder. He first sees a large red telephone with an emergency light next to it. He understands immediately that this phone's only purpose is to receive a call from the governor with an order of reprieve. Even Gacy, in the throes of delusion, doesn't believe he will hear that phone ring. He realizes that nobody will issue a rain check for this ballgame.

His eyes trail down below the phone. On a metal desk sits what appears to be a control box with tentacle-like intravenous lines and electrical cords emanating from the back. In large black letters are the words, *Override*, *Phase*, and *Armed*.

Not sure what those labels signify, Gacy then reads the words off to the right of the machine: *Start* and *Finish*. This, he understands ...

19.

GIFT GIVING ON DEATH ROW

I was staring out my office window late in the afternoon. Winter is a long, gloomy time in Chicago, but February, the shortest on the calendar, always seems the longest. It is dark when you go to work and dark when you leave to come home. The weather is particularly cold and bitter, and the seasonal novelty of snow has long passed. Whatever accumulation remains on the ground is dirty and gray, reminding us that winter is a stubborn malingerer. People from warmer climates always contend that Chicagoans become used to the weather. I will tell you that is not true. It's like saying you get used to root canals. Nor is it true that winter in Chicago builds character; it builds bad moods, depression, and the desire to eat and sleep to excess.

As I sat at my desk with my day's last cup of coffee in front of me, I watched the snow flurries swirl in all directions against the darkening sky and backdrop of the monolithic Sears Tower. I had just started to plan where and when the dinner and wine would happen when my direct phone line rang. A familiar prison recording announced that John Gacy was calling, asked if I would accept the call, and warned me that the call could be recorded, not for training and quality assurance, I thought.

"Hello, JW."
"Hey, Dollface."

"So, what's shaking down there on the Mississippi?"

"Shaking my dick every chance I get."

By this time, Gacy felt free to be rude and crude with me, and I could match his bluntness word for word. It may not be my best quality, but I am rarely offended by words.

"Remember, I'm your last lawyer, John. When you're nothing but a jar of ashes, don't come running to me."

"Ha! So, when are ya coming to see me?"

"Such a long way, John, and it's not like there's a welcome mat when I get there."

"I have some birthday gifts for you, Doll. You're really gonna like 'em."

I could only imagine what charming, hand-picked prison gifts my killer client had selected for me. "Have you been out shopping at Saks without telling the warden?"

"Nothing but the best for you, Babe."

Gacy didn't grovel, but he wanted the visit. He had been angling for me to go down there for several weeks. There was no real reason for a face-to-face meeting, but knowing the man was locked up in a cesspool with 50 of his closest condemned killers swarming around him with at most 150 days left to live, it was hard for me to say no. By the end of the call, I had promised to be down at Menard the following Tuesday.

Greg wasn't able to make this trip with me, and he suggested I bring my young associate attorney, Ellen, for two purposes: One, strength in numbers, and two, to give her the experience of a lifetime.

Ellen had just graduated the prior June with not only a law degree but a Master's in Business. She was tall, beautiful, and smart, and like most young lawyers, did not intend to work in a small firm for any length of time. Once she gained experience, she would probably move on to a bigger and better opportunity when it presented itself.

Greg and I knew this and always did our best to provide training and guidance for these young jurists because it was the right thing to do and created goodwill for years thereafter. Many lawyers whom I mentored over the years continue to reach out and thank me for the experience, sometimes with words and other times with business referrals. Surprisingly, when I mentioned the trip to Menard to Ellen, she made no bones about telling me she had no interest in going. I thought curiosity would have made her at least mildly interested. A field trip to a prison is not pleasant, but it's interesting. Not wanting to be oppositional, however, Ellen agreed.

We decided to fly, rather than drive. So, on Tuesday morning, Ellen and I were on the first flight out to St. Louis, the closest big city to Menard. We took off from Midway, Chicago's smaller but busy airport on the city's near southwest side. Just before 7 a.m., we were seated on the small plane and asleep immediately. An hour and 15 minutes later, the flight attendant announced our descent into St. Louis. I looked out the window and saw the iconic "Gateway to the West" Arch, the 630'-tall stainless-steel monument sitting on the western bank of the Mississippi River. I had fond memories of taking the tram up to the top during an educational trip with my family when I was ten.

The plane touched down smoothly, and with little delay we were headed toward our rental car to make our way to Menard, about an hour and 15-minute trip.

Ellen, who hailed from Miami, had not spent much time in the heartland of rural Illinois and was amazed at the number of cows, barns, and not a whole lot of anything along the way. The scenery was barren and gray. The cornfields had been stripped and the land turned over to await spring planting. When we came within sight of the Mississippi, Ellen was astounded that this was the same river into which she had vomited on a youthfully decadent college excursion to New Orleans for Mardi Gras. Almost six hours from the time I left my house, we pulled into the Menard Correctional Center parking lot, the plane trip door to door being almost the same as the trip by car.

By now, I was a death row regular. The prison did not have many female attorneys visiting inmates. And probably none with a red suit and three-inch matching heels. Ellen was about 5'10" with long, brown hair and shapely athletic legs emanating from her light blue wool suit. She was perpetually tan from trips home to Miami, and I knew that we were in for lots of attention. We made our way to the reception desk where two tall male guards were drinking coffee and chewing something—tobacco or gum, I knew not which. Ogling us lazily, one turned to the other and said in that languorous Southern Illinois accent, "Proof in the living flesh that JW is rehabilitated."

Realizing he meant that Gacy had given up his homosexual ways for us, I smiled and replied, "He's just our type: a man in uniform with a big insurance policy and a short lifespan." Death row humor had become second nature.

After the standard body search that pleased the guards to no end, we embarked on the winding trip to death row through the maze of doors and hallways. I had to make sure that Ellen was okay, and it helped my nerves to attend to her nerves. When the hoots and hollers began, they were even louder and more vulgar with two women and no man as a potential shield. While waiting in one vestibule, I turned to Ellen, whose normal poise had taken a beating. "And you said it was hard to meet single men."

When we reached the death row office, the guards spent an inordinate amount of time taking in Ellen's appearance and seemed to find some nonexistent tasks that needed to be accomplished before we were released from captivity into the wild of the visitors' jungle. We saw Gacy in his usual cubicle, handcuffed and talking animatedly to another inmate.

"Who is that talking to Gacy?" I asked the guard whose big frame was nearest to me, but whose eyes were staring down Ellen's blouse into her tanned cleavage.

"That's Andy Kokoraleis, one of the Ripper Crew. Better watch your lady parts," he laughed.

The Ripper Crew was a satanic cult composed of serial killers, cannibals, rapists, and necrophiliacs, including the man staring at us through the thick glass. This group of miscreants was suspected of the disappearance of 18 women in Illinois in 1981 and 1982. When interrogated, Andrew's brother, Thomas, confessed that he and the others had taken women to their "satanic chapel" where they raped and tortured them, amputated their breasts, and ate parts of them while masturbating. Andrew was convicted of only two of the murders and was sentenced to death.

The guard continued, "Those two get on pretty good seein' how they like to compare notes with each other."

I said, "You know what they say about being judged by the company you keep." By his facial expression, I doubted he understood my humor.

I looked over at Ellen whose otherwise normally tanned face had turned ashen, and there were lines of fear etched on her forehead. While the guards were creepy and Gacy was not a choir boy, these men seemed safe compared to Mr. Kokoraleis.

With a loud buzz causing Ellen to jump, the heavy door opened and we were in the pen, the door locking behind us. Kokoraleis studied us with a dull smile as our client introduced him as his "bud Koko." Just as it was with Gacy, peering into the eyes of someone who committed such inhuman acts is surreal. It is hard to believe you are dealing with the same species.

"You need anything while you're here, you let me know," Koko said in a monotone voice. Wondering vaguely what a man who amputates and eats breasts could do for me, I gave him a tight smile.

He was the last inmate executed before Illinois abolished the death penalty in 2011. On the day of his execution, one politician, staunchly against the death penalty his whole life, said, "What this gentleman did, I can't object to what the Governor did." Interestingly, one of the Ripper Crew members recently completed his sentence and is living in Aurora, Illinois, a town you may wish to remove from your Spring Break list.

I turned to Gacy and formally introduced him to Ellen. For about ten minutes, we made small talk. When you visit prisoners, you soon realize they are almost always interested in the outdoors, the weather, the details of your trip, and the goings-on in a world they left behind many years ago. Gacy was no different, and he had all kinds of questions about the airport, the plane, St. Louis, and the kind of car we rented.

He immediately discovered that Ellen was from Florida, and they chatted about some of the places he had traveled in the state on business. I wondered vaguely what non-employment-related atrocities Gacy may have committed in the Sunshine State.

Gacy was his usual, gregarious, curious, and talkative self. In my role as the death row vending machine footman, I took his junk food order: two Baby Ruth bars and two Diet Cokes. As I got up, Ellen immediately volunteered to accompany me, clearly not comfortable being alone with our client. I would have advised her to stay with the devil you know versus the devil you don't, but she was already out of the cubicle and on my heels.

I bought Gacy's treats and Diet Coke for the girls. When we returned, Gacy stood up to acknowledge our return, ironically in the manner of a true gentleman.

Ellen attempted to kid around. "John, with all that sugar in your candy bars, you still like the Diet Coke, huh?"

"Ya know, I just like the taste of it, always have. The sugar in my candy? Gotta die of something."

I couldn't fault him for his love of the stuff. When I was in college, I could polish off a good amount of gooey fattening pizza, but God forbid you try to serve me a real Coke. His sugar hypocrisy seemed one of the most normal things about him.

Just after we began to relax 15 minutes into our conversation, I experienced my most frightening moment on death row. As I was sitting across the metal desk from Gacy with my back turned toward the entrance to the cubicle, I heard a sudden shuffling. Out of the corner of my eye, I saw a gangly inmate lunge into our space.

"Matches!" he screamed. "Matches. You got matches?"

Three things happened to me at once. I jumped out of my seat. I propelled myself back from the desk. I almost wet myself. A 6'1" inmate was standing inches away from me, his shaking hands extended, as if to grab us. His disheveled hair alone would have made him look deranged, but his eyes were what terrified me. They were bright clear blue, wide open, unblinking, and completely vacant. Manson eyes. The eyes of a psychotic person in a manic state. The eyes of someone who was out of control.

I would later learn that our unexpected visitor was Tom Odle, the youngest man ever on Illinois death row. He was just 18 years old when he entered his family home in central Illinois and in a rage strangled and stabbed to death his mother, father, 14-year-old sister, and two brothers, ages 13 and 10. Mr. Odle's motive in killing his entire family? They were "constantly jumping on (sic) my throat," apparently for playing his music too loud.

Gacy stood up, coughed politely, and calmly replied, "Listen, Tom. I ain't got no stinking matches." Looking pleased with his play on the line from the movie *The Treasure of Sierra Madre*, he gracefully raised his hands (cuffed together) and gestured to us. "And neither do these ladies. Would you please do us a favor and let us get back to our meeting?"

Odle furtively peered at us, well, through us. With a confused frown, he skipped backward and proceeded to the next cubicle to repeat his frantic request. To my knowledge, arson was at least one crime Odle had yet to commit in his young life, but I nevertheless felt uncomfortable knowing he was trying to get his quivering hands on some matches. Who knew that John Wayne Gacy could act as my protector?

Feeling like I needed a break, I offered to go back to the vending machine for supplemental provisions. This time Gacy wanted a Snickers bar and some peanut butter cheese crackers. I filled his order and bought us all another Diet Coke. When I returned, he was in the process of picking up two parcels wrapped in brown paper that had been propped against the wall of the cubicle. It was some type of artwork, and I had a good guess the artist was not Claude Monet.

"Time for your birthday gifts, Dollface."

I had no idea how he knew my birthday was the following week. I had heard quite a bit about Gacy's artistic talents. "Aw, JW. You shouldn't have. Hope there's a gift receipt in case I don't like it." *Hopefully, the return policy extends past May 10*, I thought.

I began unwrapping the first masterpiece. Gacy, in his usual loquacious manner, rattled on about how he was a prodigious artist, painting all day when he wasn't reading and answering mail, working on his legal matters, or seeing visitors. He started painting in the nude years ago because it was so hot during the summer. He soon realized that he was more creative while naked, not to mention spillage being less of a problem. So now, he always painted while unclothed.

"I cannot unsee that, John," I said.

When the paper fell to the floor, I held up my gift for all to see. Hmm.

"It's called *Skull Clown*," said John proudly.

And that's exactly what it was. A crudely painted skull with a clown's hat perched jauntily on top. Signed for authentication purposes. So much goes through a person's mind. Could anyone ever hang something like this on the wall? Can keeping a painting in your home haunt it? Would someone pay money for this crap? Will the Salvation Army take this kind of thing?

According to Gacy, he painted numerous versions of this subject because it was the most in demand. The second most popular painting was his self-portrait, *Pogo the Clown,* which depicts him in full clown gear holding balloons and waving slyly to the beholder. He also painted many variations of the Seven Dwarfs, which has ruined forever my childhood memory of watching the Walt Disney classic *Snow White.*

"Well, thank you, John. I like this and will treasure it." I was careful wrapping it up tightly. "What's next?" I asked, feigning eagerness.

"This is one that I painted specially for you. No one has this one. It's unique."

I could only imagine. I ceremoniously stripped off the paper and there, before my eyes, was a horrible blue and purple ... seascape?

He blurted out its title, "*Ebony Sea*!"

"Of course, that's what it is! Wow. Very impressive.

Where did you get the idea for this one?"

"I think of the world as dark and mysterious, kind of like me."

"Well, thanks, John. I think you're a talented painter."

Knowing that Gacy was a housepainter in his freedom years, I wanted to add my advice that he should stay away from canvases and stick to houses.

...

Around lunchtime, I saw other inmates getting their lunch trays. Gacy broke it to us gently that he had been required to give up his lunch for another inmate who was hosting a guest a few stalls down. So, there would be no formal lunch, which would require us to go back to the vending machines for sustenance.

Several Milk Duds and Hershey bars later, we started talking about cooking. Interestingly, because Gacy was in the company of two women, I noticed his mannerisms and speech patterns had become slightly softer and more feminine. His conversations, too, became chatty and girly.

Gacy bragged about how he was a great cook, having worked in the kitchen of the Iowa prison and at Bruno's in the early 70s. He talked about how he experimented with new recipes and followed some his mother had taught him growing up. He was really into it. Ellen was intrigued by Gacy's interest in cooking and his attention to the detail of certain spices and ingredients he was describing.

"Too bad you can't cook while you're in here, John," Ellen commiserated.

With mock shock, he replied, "Of course, I still cook. Don't you know about commissary cuisine?"

Blank faces from the lawyers.

He went on to describe recipes that could be concocted from food commonly available at prison commissaries and were well-known in prisons across the country. For instance, Prison Pad Thai was made from a package of ramen noodles, a jar of peanut butter, a bag of peanuts, and hot sauce. His favorite was Hard Time Tamales. I still remember it. You take a bag of corn chips, a bag of cheese curls, beef jerky, and ½ cup of warm water. Crush it all together into the chip bag and shape it into a tamale. Run it under hot water to cook. Open up the bag and "¡Fantastico!"

Six hours after we arrived, Ellen and I found ourselves winding our way back to the prison entrance, our lives enhanced by six Diet Cokes between us, two wall hangings of questionable taste, and in the case of Ellen, the satisfaction of having many new male admirers. As we buckled ourselves into our rental car, we agreed to stay overnight in St. Louis before flying home.

Just as I predicted, in the next two weeks, Ellen received at least five handwritten letters from various Menard residents who had used their vast free time and limited resources to find her name and address. Three were invitations to visit. One was a profession of lust. Another one began with an argument for why she should be his lawyer and ended with a description of how his memory of her helped him reach sexual gratification. That had to count for something, I told her.

She said, "Next time you get one of these, you have my permission to shred it."

One week after Gacy was executed, Ellen politely expressed her appreciation for the job, left our firm with four days' notice, and moved back to Miami. She never practiced criminal law again. In fact, she stopped litigating and, to this day, writes estate plans for retired Floridians.

On her last day of work, Ellen told me in parting she had taken the pretty blue suit she had worn to see Gacy and threw it down her apartment building's garbage chute.

20.

CLOWNS GET AWAY WITH MURDER

When I arrived home from my trip, I flopped down on the couch with my coat still on. I unwrapped my two Gacy paintings and placed them on my coffee table for viewing. My cat, who had been circling my legs from the time I walked in the door, jumped on the table. He sniffed the canvases, looked at me dismissively, jumped down, and scampered away.

I have a theory about home decorating. When you buy a piece of furniture, art, or a knickknack and take it home, it will find its way to where it belongs. The house will tell you. After rewrapping the paintings, I walked straight downstairs to my basement, placed them in the far corner of the storage room, and covered them with a painting tarp. I completely forgot about them until many years later when I sold the house. When I was packing, I stumbled upon them and realized that I had unknowingly placed them next to the area that accessed my home's crawlspace. It seemed those paintings wanted to be right where they ended up.

Before Gacy died, he gifted me a third painting, *Pogo the Clown*, a very popular item for which collectors of strange art and serial killer memorabilia clamored. People could not get enough of his clown art. When you think about it, Gacy's lasting legacy, other than the trail of destruction surrounding his murders, is his reputation as a clown.

Clowns have always been creepy—they are people whose

identities are hidden by disguise, happy faces painted garishly, playing pranks on kids. Gacy brought this creepiness to new heights. Many people wrongly think he got away with his crimes by posing as a clown. In fact, he was in plain clothing when he picked up the boys and men he killed. He lured his victims by looking like a normal guy—a union steward, a truck driver, a bowling alley manager.

People who wear lurid make-up, clown noses, and floppy shoes cannot ensnare innocent young men and boys into their cars and homes. He looked and acted like your average guy, your blue-collar uncle who plops himself in the Lazy Boy to watch football after Thanksgiving dinner. That is how he got away with murder.

No, Gacy's clowning was done in his free time—that is, when he wasn't working construction or engaged in his industrious killing spree.

In the early 1970s, he joined a local Moose Club, which had a "Jolly Joker" clown club whose members, dressed as clowns, would regularly perform at fundraisers, parties, and parades in addition to volunteering to entertain hospitalized children.

Interestingly, as many times as he told the world that he had engaged in these charitable activities, there is no evidence that he attended any one such event. It is true that by late 1975, Gacy had created his performance character, Pogo the Clown, a name fashioned from his Polish heritage and the fact that he was always "on the go." He said he designed his costumes and taught himself how to apply clown makeup. He was known to have frequented a favorite Chicago drinking venue named "The Good Luck Lounge" in full costume, telling patrons he had just performed as Pogo and was stopping for a social drink before heading home. It is more likely he was lying about his performance and simply wanted people to see him dressed up this way. He was very proud of his clowning and saw absolutely nothing odd about the hobby.

Several days after the Gacy art was stored safely in my basement and I had sent a handwritten thank you card to my incarcerated benefactor—good etiquette should be followed despite the circumstances—I was on the phone with him. He asked me where I had decided to hang his paintings. I mumbled something about waiting to find just the right spot and then quickly changed the subject to the topic of clowns.

"I've been meaning to ask you, JW. What's up with the clown obsession? You seem to identify with clowns."

His voice changed to its softer-edged version, and he became animated. He told me that he had always loved clowns in the circus because they were so sneaky. They were always "up to no good," and kids just didn't expect them to have hand buzzers, flowers appearing from behind their backs, or water squirting from their noses. He told me he was very careful in how he applied his clown makeup. Why he used certain colors and an upside-down grin with sharp corners rather than rounded ones. He thought the sharp corners made for a scarier appearance, which he favored.

Of course, he did.

He went into great detail about his oil-based grease paint and how he used white face powder over the white makeup and translucent powder over the bright colors to set the makeup in place. It was strictly unprofessional for a clown's makeup to run during a performance. It was like listening to a cosmetics lesson from an evil Estee Lauder.

At times, Gacy was "good, happy Pogo" and at others, he was "sad, evil Pogo." I asked him how he chose between the two. That was simple, he explained. It depended upon how the children he was entertaining behaved and whether they were good or bad. (I loved hearing how John Wayne Gacy was an arbiter of the morality of children.) When kids were polite and non-aggressive at parties and parades, he handed out candy with a smile. But if the children were greedy and reached for more, he would pinch them hard, swear at them, and threaten to kill them. When the child screamed and cried to his parents, he would deny what he had done. He always got away with it, according to him, because "clowns get away with murder."

Not to get too deep into the psychology of a person who dresses up as a clown, but I believe Gacy's clowning was a bit more profound than what appeared on the surface.

Social psychologist Phil Zimbardo performed fascinating studies indicating that there are specific situations that make nearly all people engage in behaviors that are deemed "evil," and others that facilitate socially acceptable behavior. According to him, one of the most important variables that predicts anti-social behavior is "deindividuation," a state where a person's identity is hidden.

People in online anonymous chat rooms are deindividuated as are people at costume parties. Individuals in this state are more likely to hurt others, cheat, steal, lie, and even kill. The history of war shows that soldiers wear uniforms and masks to take away their individuality, thereby making it easier for them to battle enemies. Think about anonymous telemarketers who rudely press on without regard for politeness. How website comments are nastier than anything people would say in person. How killers in slasher films like *Halloween* and *Friday the 13th* wear masks. Why clowns are creepy: When you lack a clear identity, morality is up for grabs.

Gacy was undoubtedly evil before he started dressing up as a clown. Whatever train wreck that occurred in his childhood had already been set in motion long before he donned the Bozo nose. But could it be that his clown get-up was one of the ways he deindividuated himself through anonymity, which allowed him to "punish" naughty children? And was this alternating display of magnanimity and retribution something he learned from his capricious alcoholic father? And when he dressed up in circus attire, did this allow his already weak moral code to disappear like a coin behind a clown's ear?

21.

A MAN'S WORLD

In the 14 years that Gacy's legal matters ran up and down through the state and federal courts, he had many excellent lawyers. They were from large firms, mid-sized firms, and solo practices. They were of different ages and backgrounds. They were diverse in many ways except, to my knowledge, none was a female. When I represented Gacy, it was clear that I was being treated very differently than my three male counterparts. I think it's important to talk about the constant tug of discrimination, harassment, and disparate treatment that weighed me down throughout my career and likely does the same to many women in their professions.

I started law school in 1983 at the University of Illinois College of Law, an excellent state school in the cornfields of Illinois in Champaign. At orientation, we were told proudly by our dean that our class of law students was the first that was 50% female. Despite this great statistic, when thrown into the sea of the working world, I learned my treatment was anything but even-handed.

I want to be clear: I like being a woman. I know that being a woman makes me different than a man. I do not want to dress like a man, talk like a man, or really even think like a man. There is no such thing as being treated the same as a man because we are not the same. Not only is our plumbing plumbed differently, but our wiring is wired differently. I believe strongly that women excel in ways that are different than men. They should not only be proud of this, but they should also exploit it for all it is worth.

According to gender disparity expert, attorney, and author Andrea Kramer, there are certain organizational constructs, corporate practices, and patterns of interaction that have been the cause of inequality in the workplace. Women were not admitted to the bar until 1922. Why? In many states, women were not permitted to enter into contracts without their husbands' consent, and therefore, they were unable to enter into a retention agreement with clients.

In 1872, The U.S. Supreme Court heard the case of Myra Blackwell, an Illinois woman who had graduated from law school but was denied admittance to the bar by the highest court in Illinois. She argued to the Supreme Court that the 14th Amendment protected her equal rights.

Justice Joseph Bradley, in finding that women were not fit to become lawyers, stated, "Man is, or should be, woman's protector and defender. The natural and proper timidity and delicacy which belongs to the female sex evidently unfits it for many of the occupations of civil life ... The paramount destiny and mission of women are to fulfill the noble and benign offices of wife and mother. This is the law of the Creator," or some such bullshit.

Seven years later, President Hayes signed a law that allowed women to argue before the Supreme Court, but it took much longer for states to finally permit women to practice in their courts.

Amazingly, it wasn't until 1920 that women were allowed to practice law in all states. Even when the rules changed, many law firms and chambers still cited a lack of female toilets as a justifiable barrier to employing women. While women have clearly come a long way, on average female legal professionals are still paid less than their male counterparts, and while law school attendance records show gender equality, the number of female lawyers in practice is only 37%.

By the time I met Greg, I had been treated shabbily in my

many prior employment situations. Lawyers and judges asked me repeatedly in court and at depositions if I was the court reporter.

While I was an associate attorney in a Chicago firm, I went on a business trip with a partner. He hit on me aggressively, and I knew he had asked me to accompany him for reasons other than my legal prowess. When we arrived at the hotel front desk, he told me there was only one room available, leaving me standing at the front desk stunned. The clerk motioned me over to reassure me there were plenty of rooms, so I used my own credit card to pay for one.

On another occasion, I was trying a case for a female client who had been sexually assaulted and locked in a restaurant cooler by her boss. During jury selection, the 75-year-old judge, who they called out of retirement due to a crowded docket, made repeated sexually suggestive comments to me in front of the jury pool.

He told the jury that he wanted me to come back in chambers and have a sidebar with me on his lap, that he liked his women barefoot and pregnant, and that it was a real pleasure to work with a lawyer who had nice legs.

I was worried that the jury would not take my client's allegations seriously because of the judge's horrible comments, so I settled the case before we gave opening statements. After the jury was dismissed, several of the female jurors rushed over and told me they were so incensed about the judge's harassment that they would have given my client "a million dollars." Suffice to say, I settled for much less than a million.

While I was an associate at one of Chicago's most prestigious large firms, my boss told me that he didn't want me to work on cases that involved litigation because it would impact my "lifestyle." I had specifically chosen this firm because I wanted to be a litigator, so I was puzzled.

He explained, "You know. You're going to want to get married and have children, and the litigator's lifestyle is going to get in the way."

In some regard, this man was trying to be kind, but of course this was textbook sexual discrimination. According to expert Andrea Kramer, this particular brand of disparate treatment is known as "benevolent gender bias." It results from an assumption that women need to be protected, directed, and assisted by men and leads to women receiving devalued projects. This in turn leads to a lack of notable achievements and promotions.

When I joined forces with Greg, he protected me from much of this treatment. There were clients of our firm who preferred him as the testosterone-wielding, macho litigator and those who preferred my hand-holding and collaborative negotiating skills.

We used the yin and the yang to our advantage and to that of our clients. Just when I thought the gender issues were mostly behind me, the Supreme Court happened.

In October 1991, Greg and I handled a case for the Cook County Democratic Party against the Harold Washington Party, the county's first African American party named after our first mayor of color. The issue involved complicated issues of ballot access.

When we agreed to handle the case pro bono, we assumed it would not involve much work because the election that raised the issues had already occurred, so we believed the issues to be moot.

Shortly after filing our Petition for Writ of Certiorari, in which we asked the U.S. Supreme Court to further consider the matter, we received word that it had granted our Petition, and the case would be set for oral argument. The Court only hears 165 cases per year, which is 2.5% of all cases that are petitioned to be heard. Our case was not only one of them, it was scheduled for argument on the first Monday of October, the first day of the Court's term. It is thought that the Court hears what it considers the most important cases of the term on that day. We were off to Washington, D.C.!

To handle a case and sit at the table for arguments before our nation's highest court, you are required to have practiced at least three years and must apply for special admission. I had been practicing for five years. I had long ago submitted my paperwork and had received my approval and Supreme Court bar certificate.

Our case was set for argument in the afternoon. All lawyers who were scheduled to argue cases waited in the library until the afternoon session opened. Ten minutes before Court opened, the Court Clerk, suited in a formal morning coat, tails hanging behind him, led all ten of us to the gate leading to the area where the lawyers' tables awaited.

A few minutes before show time, the Clerk ceremoniously opened the gate, and in we marched to our tables. I was the only female.

We waited nervously for several minutes in deafening silence, taking in the stately courtroom decor. The walls and ceiling were paneled in rich oak, and stunning chandeliers hung high over our heads. A heavy red velvet curtain draped behind the justices' empty seats, waiting to be filled by some of the most intelligent jurists in the country.

Suddenly, a bell rang, and from behind the curtain, the justices emerged onto the elevated platform like racehorses from a gate. In unison, they were seated in their high-backed chairs. Instead of the usual nine justices, there were only eight.

Just one month before, Justice Thurgood Marshall, the Court's first African American, had retired. President George H. W. Bush nominated Clarence Thomas to replace him. That day, at that very time a few blocks away, the Senate was conducting hearings on Thomas' fitness to serve on the Court.

In a historic and bizarre display of questioning, it was alleged that Thomas had sexually harassed women, including a Yale-educated law professor named Anita Hill. This happened at least partly during the time Thomas served as Chairman of the Equal Employment Opportunity Commission—the very body tasked with protecting minorities in the workplace, including women.

Millions of television viewers watched as Hill was questioned by the Senate (led by then-Senator Joe Biden) about her allegations that Thomas talked to her about large-breasted women, a porn star named Long Dong Silver, and a pubic hair on a Coke can. Not your everyday Senate hearing subject matter. Hills' testimony was the first time I recall a woman speaking so publicly about workplace harassment, something that so many have experienced.

There I was facing the eight justices, seated on their lofty bench peering down at us. Chief Justice Rehnquist was particularly intimidating. I would later describe him as having such a large forehead, it was almost a five-head.

My eyes immediately focused on Justice Sandra Day O'Connor, the first female ever to serve on the U.S. Supreme Court, another first that happened in my lifetime. Although O'Connor was 71 years of age, she was more attractive and youthful in person. Her blondish-gray hair set off her piercing blue eyes, and she was formidable despite her petite size. I surveyed the other justices, and my eyes came back to O'Connor. To my horror, she was staring and pointing at me. With her head, she motioned to a clerk standing behind her. He leaned down, and the Justice whispered in his ear, still glaring right at me. I felt like a schoolgirl caught passing a note.

The clerk looked up at me with a stern expression and disappeared behind the Oz-like curtain. I turned to Greg, who shrugged his shoulders as if to say, "Beats the hell out of me."

The justices remained on the bench in silence, several glancing at me. Nothing was happening. Within a minute, O'Connor's clerk came up from behind me. He leaned down, tapped me gently on the shoulder, and whispered in a voice everyone could hear, "Excuse me, but are you a member of the Supreme Court bar?"

Now, I told you: The procedure to become a member of this bar was the most formal one in the country. I was required to procure signatures from judges attesting to my fitness and character. I had to have two members of the Supreme Court bar vouch for my good standing and morality. I wrote a personal statement, swore under oath to follow the rules, and paid a fee. After waiting many weeks, I finally received a formal certificate that was signed and embossed by the Clerk. To enter the courthouse that day, I was asked to show my bar admission paperwork and two pieces of identification. I signed a document stating I was there on official business, to argue a Supreme Court case. There was no question the Court was expecting me because my name had been printed on the booklets listing the cases on the docket that day. The clerk's questioning of me led me to one conclusion: Justice Sandra Day O'Connor believed I was an imposter.

I turned in my seat and looked up at him. "Yes, Sir. I am a member of the bar. I submitted my application two months ago and received my certificate in September."

The courier straightened up and nodded to the bench. O'Connor nodded back, seemingly relieved. Did she think I was impersonating a Supreme Court lawyer?

That experience shook me. I could not believe that the first and only female justice on the highest court of the land—a veritable branch of government—had singled me out to verify my right to be there. Why did this happen? I probably looked young, but I did not look any younger than my 29 years. I was dressed in a staid black suit. I was conducting myself seriously, professionally, and with respect for where I was. It's clear. She did this because of my gender. But why? It could be that less than one percent of all attorneys arguing before the Court that year were women. Even now, only 18% of Supreme Court lawyers are women.

But O'Connor was used to being an anomaly as she had suffered serious discrimination at the beginning of her career. After graduating third in her class from Stanford Law School, she had such difficulty finding a job that the only position she could find was as a legal secretary. She offered to work with no pay for a deputy county attorney in California, and even then, they didn't allow her to perform legal work for the first few weeks.

And she did this to me?

Many years later, I sat at dinner with O'Connor at an event in the Illinois' capitol to honor the first woman to practice law in our state. She was perfectly charming, but I had to bite my tongue not to ask her why this had happened. I still have the program from that event. It contains a quote from the woman who singled me out in the Supreme Court: "Society, as a whole, benefits immeasurably from a climate in which all persons, regardless of race or gender, may have the opportunity to earn respect, responsibility, advancement and remuneration based on ability."

Well said, Ms. Justice. *I hope we can now put those words into action.*

When these types of events occur in a woman's life, the collective result is that, sometimes, a little voice whispers in your ear, "Hey! Are you sure you are supposed to be here?"

Fortunately for me, I am hard of hearing when it comes to these little voices, but I imagine many women do listen and that this is one of the reasons so many drop out of the profession. I think of these experiences like pebbles in the shoe of my career: They bother me a little, but they don't stop me from moving forward.

Now we come to the time of the Gacy representation. As I said earlier, the vast majority of hate mail, death threats, and weird missives were directed at me, the sole female on the team. That could have been in part because I had assumed the Gacy spokesperson role. Even so, the vitriol was more vicious, frequent, and personal when it came to me. I should have saved the hundreds of communications I received because they were as frightening as they were colorful and as creative as they were disturbing. I shudder to think if there had been social media when I represented Gacy! From the content and tone of these messages, I conclude that there is a perception that female lawyers are weaker and more susceptible to criticism, which causes the communication bullies of the world to think they have an easier mark.

I also believe the public found it more offensive for a woman to be doing a man's job in a difficult case. Rather than respecting a strong woman's role in a high-profile case, many people, especially women, were highly critical of me—my femininity or lack thereof, clothing, makeup, and other physical and personal attributes. One woman wrote to tell me my hair needed conditioner and went on to describe how I looked like a Barbie Doll that had gone through a washing machine (points for creativity).

Many of the letters I received were of a sexual nature. To

me, this implies that when many people see a woman in a public setting, they feel the need to sexualize her.

One cretin wrote to tell me they knew that I was actually a man in disguise, and another accused me of being Gacy's lover. A woman from Canada had a convoluted theory that I operated a prostitution ring that was getting publicity due to my association with this infamous client. And my favorite is the claim that I was Gacy's brainwashed automaton, blindly doing his bidding even after his death, like a serial killer Stepford Wife.

These missives continue to this day and, although many of them are humorous, they remind me to watch my back.

22.

SEX TALK WITH A SERIAL KILLER

March in Chicago causes fatigue in even the most weather-resistant folks. Even if the Groundhog promises a quick spring, Chicagoans know the rodent lies.

I arrived at my office early that Monday. I was dressed down because the courts were closed for Casimir Pulaski Day, a holiday observed in Illinois on the first Monday of March. Pulaski was a Revolutionary War cavalry officer born in Poland and praised for his contributions in the American Revolution. Casimir Pulaski Day is celebrated in Chicago due to its large Polish population. Twenty percent of Chicagoans are of Polish descent, and the city is home to the largest number of Polish immigrants in the U.S. Today, Polish is the third most common language spoken in Chicago, behind English and Spanish.

I remembered suddenly that Gacy had spoken with pride about having been appointed director of Chicago's Polish Day Parade in 1975. He described the hard work that went into organizing the parade and encouraging politicians, local Polish restaurants, and businesses to assemble floats. It was through his work with the Polish Day festivities that Gacy met and was photographed with First Lady Rosalynn Carter. It is one of the most frequently published photos of him because it symbolizes his importance and respect in the community.

When Gacy was arrested, the Secret Service was pressed

on how he could have access to the president's wife. On his lapel was a pin denoting the Secret Service had cleared him.

When an investigation finally got to the bottom of it, the answer was simple: Gacy was in charge of security for the event and was automatically given a pass. Members of the Chicago Democratic Party knew Gacy would have direct contact with Rosalynn Carter, even though Gacy had several arrest records for felonious sexual assault by that time, with one of those arrests being just a few months prior. It begs the question: If Gacy was allowed that much privilege, even considering his arrests, how much did people in power know about his crimes? I often wonder how often Mrs. Carter saw that picture and rued the day she came into contact with Gacy.

As I looked out my window at the tall buildings crowding the skyline on a backdrop of deceivingly bright blue sky, I thought I should call Gacy to see how he might be celebrating Pulaski Day behind bars. He must have read my mind because, at that moment, the intercom buzzed, and my secretary announced the prison call.

I picked up the phone. "What a coincidence. Just getting ready to call the Polish Prince himself. Happy Pulaski Day, JW."

He paused. Maybe the prison wasn't serving pierogis, and he had forgotten about the holiday.

"I don't mean Roman Polanski, John."

I thought he may not have gotten my reference to the disgraced film director who fled the country after being convicted of having sex with a minor, but Gacy blurted out, "Polanski, now that guy is a sicko."

"Aren't you judgmental today, John."

Gacy, never at a loss for tasteless but topical jokes, said, "Speaking of Polish: Why don't Polish women use vibrators?"

"Hmm."

"It chips their teeth."

"That conversation went downhill fast, John, but now that you're talking about sex first thing on a Monday morning, I have a question for you."

The weekend before I was reading some materials from the psychiatric interviews Gacy had given prior to his trial. There were some interesting discussions about his sexual development and preferences. I had never specifically addressed these issues with him and had no legitimate reason to do so, but my curiosity got the better of me knowing some upcoming deadlines might short-circuit my ability to ask them in the future, I decided to talk sex with John Gacy.

"John, you've told me ten times that you have never kissed a man above the waist. I think I know what that means, but I want to be sure."

He was happy to answer. He explained that he was not a homosexual and clarified that he liked sex with any consenting adult (two lies in one sentence). But, when he had sex with men, it was just to "get off" and not about emotions and love. He went on to tell me that he had considered being a priest when he was in his teens because "I didn't have no sex drive," and, "I could help people by accepting their sins and their differences."

(Can you imagine Father John having access to young male parishioners?)

I wondered if Gacy viewed the priesthood as a way of avoiding various urges he experienced with the benefit of sidestepping the expectation that he would marry a woman.

It also made me think of the growing web of political connections he had: During a period when anything but vanilla sex was brutally rejected by mainstream public opinion, had Gacy told men who wanted to have high-flying political careers they could have it both ways and he could accept "their sins and differences?"

Sadly, I never had the chance to ask him directly about this. However, in the legal documents filed after his incarceration, he provided an inventory of his house to the court. Therein he specifically lists blackmail files in his office as "private list of known homo politicians, sports figures, county and city employees." Where those files went is a complete unknown.

Gacy admitted to me he was shy about sex when he was a teenager. He described his first experience at 18 when he was "necking" in a car with some "broad" and he passed out while taking off her clothing. He said it surprised him that he was apparently not interested enough to complete the act and wondered if there was something wrong with him. He switched topics after that.

He told me his mother sat him down while he was in his teens and told him "all about sex." She told him that sex with your wife was one of God's miracles and was a "beautiful thing." She told him he had to be gentle, and it was not about immediate gratification, but a way to communicate your feelings and emotions. The most important thing was to make sure your wife was satisfied before you were. That would make a good, long-lasting marriage.

Gacy told me his first experience with the "broad in the car" confused him because, instead of thinking of that first experience as beautiful and religious in nature, all he could recall was feelings of disgust and disinterest. It seems this is what caused the blackout—a way to avoid the act.

Interestingly, Gacy's two wives said consistently that he was a kind and gentle lover and that there was nothing violent or rough about sex with him. His second wife, Carol, referred to marital relations with him as "very gentle, very warm."

Although Gacy was the one to initiate the encounters, he was never forceful or demanding. That part of their life was, at first, very happy and satisfying. Carol did, however, recall the sickeningly sweet smell that seemed to emanate from the crawlspace below their bedroom. Can you imagine looking back and thinking you were married to someone who was torturing, raping, and killing boys during the same time he was sleeping with you? And that your lovemaking was happening in a room positioned directly over the decaying bodies? Gacy told his psychiatrist that during his second marriage he had completely lost interest in sex with women.

Carol discovered homosexual pornography and concluded John was no longer interested in women. When confronted, Gacy explained that his 12–20-hour days at work exhausted him. Carol first confronted him about having extramarital sex with women, but he denied it. When she then accused him of having sex with men, he told her he was not a homosexual, did not like homosexuals, and thought they were "weak and sick."

On Mother's Day 1975, Gacy announced he was not going to have sex with her again and declared the marriage was over. He told me that he had loved his two wives, that they were good women, and that "it just didn't work out."

Carol went on to say that until Gacy went to prison they continued to see each other and when he was arrested, she was completely in the dark about the murders.

There was one strange thing that popped out to her upon reflection: At one point, Gacy refurbished their house so that Carol didn't have access to several rooms, including the kitchen. He was likely blocking Carol from discovering evidence of his atrocities.

I turned the conversation around a little at this point. I again brought up the fact that there was a woman who used to tell the press that she was madly in love with Gacy and wanted to marry him. "What's the deal with that, John? What about you is so attractive to all the hot-blooded housewives out there? Is it the man in uniform thing?"

He explained, "She wasn't the only broad who fell in love with me. Women throw themselves at me so much that all the guys in here are jealous of me. It's the whole bad boy thing. If you like bad boys and you believe the media hype about me, I'm a real prize."

There is actually a word for people, mostly women, who have a sexual interest in and attraction to those who commit crimes. Hybristophilia, or the "Bonnie and Clyde syndrome," drives women to send fan mail to high-profile criminals, particularly those who have committed heinous crimes. Erik and Lyle Menendez, who were convicted of murdering their wealthy parents, both got married while in prison. The "Night Stalker," Richard Ramirez, guilty of 13 murders, multiple rapes, and child abuse, had scores of women who wrote to him and visited him regularly. These "prison groupies" may have low self-esteem and or lack a father figure. Others believe they can change a man through their nurture and caring. Many are simply motivated to be in the media spotlight or cash in on the killer's notoriety.

Finally, psychologists say that some women see this as a perfect relationship. There can never be intimacy, sexual or otherwise, and the relationship is based upon some fantasy of being together in a future that does not exist.

Sheila Isenberg in her book, *Women Who Love Men Who Kill*, claims that most if not all of the women she studied had suffered some abuse in their past and ironically view rapists and murderers behind bars as safe and unable to hurt them.

Having represented many inmates over the years, I have seen this play out. For a brief time, my law firm performed legal services for Jeffrey MacDonald, a handsome Princeton-educated physician and Green Beret known as the "Fatal Vision Murderer."

In 1970, MacDonald's wife and two young children were brutally stabbed to death in their home on the military base at Fort Bragg.

After the Army dropped military charges, MacDonald was charged and convicted of murder in federal court. The famous author Joe McGinness wrote the bestseller *Fatal Vision*, which is fascinating and well-written, but in my view, gets the story wrong. Along with many others, I believe there is substantial and convincing evidence pointing to MacDonald's innocence in a case that is one of the most litigated murder cases in American justice history.

While in prison, MacDonald had his share of love hopefuls who believed in his innocence and wanted an ongoing relationship with him.

While I represented him, he was in a relationship with an absolutely stunning, intelligent, educated, and successful woman who spent huge amounts of time and money trying to help MacDonald. She paid for his lawyers and spent thousands of dollars flying to see him in prison. It wasn't just her desire to do good; she was really in love with MacDonald and made no bones about it. I liked her. She was otherwise perfectly normal and had many other options for boyfriends and husbands. To this day, even though I believe MacDonald was wrongfully convicted, I do not understand this woman's romantic pursuit of him.

As I said earlier, Gacy liked women. He adored his mother and sisters, and he treated me much better than any of his male lawyers. He clearly had issues with his sexuality, and certainly did not like that fact about himself. He would oscillate between expressing disgust for homosexuals and then saying he had "nothing against them" and "people should be free to fuck who they want." It was an interesting part of his personality because many of the doctors who interviewed him believed that when he was killing the men and boys, he was, in effect, killing the part of himself that he so disliked. The very thing his father had accused him of being—effeminate and weak—was what he thought he had become. And he despised that.

"So, if you ever got out of jail, who would you go for—men or women?"

His answer surprised me. "Nah, I don't wanna get outa here. They'd kill me on the street. I'm much safer in here."

"Really, John? You're okay with being in the slammer?"

He paused, so I knew he was making up his next answer. "Three hots and a cot. It's a lot easier than on the outside, and anyone I care about comes to see me. I get a lot of respect here."

I believed that Gacy was being truthful about not wanting to live outside of prison. My guess is that the stress of committing these crimes had finally taken its toll by the time of his arrest. Toward the end of his spree, the murders were escalating in frequency and viciousness. The drugs, alcohol, and fear of apprehension were way too much, even for a seasoned sociopath like him.

Those who witnessed his confession immediately after he was apprehended sensed he was relieved to end the double life he was leading. His days at Menard, while spent under deplorable conditions, were ordered, certain, and predictable.

While I am certain he wasn't squeamish about committing the murders, he probably found peace in not having the ability to plan, commit, or cover up his crimes. However, if by some fluke of the justice system, Gacy were released, he and I both knew that he would go right back to where he left off.

23.

UP TO SNUFF

Our legal filings were flying out the door. The press was trying to keep track of it all, calling us, wanting copies of the briefs, and asking if we had a chance of winning anything. Having been relegated to the job of spokesperson on the case, I was regularly confronted with the media question, "You don't dispute that Gacy committed the crimes, do you? You can't be arguing that he is innocent?"

I had to be careful how I answered, as Gacy did not like me to say that he was guilty. I soon realized he had plenty of leisure time to be an avid television watcher and newspaper reader from behind bars and had feelers on the outside of the prison reporting to him, so he knew what I was telling the press.

The statement I wanted to make was, "Of course he is guilty, but capital punishment is wrong, even for him."

However, the few times I did utter that sentiment, he would promptly be on the phone with me, roaring in my ear that as his lawyer I must tell the "truth that no one wants to hear," and declare he was innocent.

As a spokesperson for a person who is not credible, credibility is of the utmost importance. I learned quickly to sidestep those media questions and do what I was trained to do: Smile and give the press the sound bite that I wanted them to have, not what they wanted me to say. Guilt, in this case, from a legal and capital punishment sense, was irrelevant.

Gacy's position on his guilt was a moving target. After his arrest, he spontaneously confessed to his defense lawyer, Sam Amirante, with a sense of relief, "I've been the judge, jury, and executioner of many people, now I want to be my judge, jury, and executioner."

What followed was a long, late-night recitation in which he recounted in intricate detail where he had met his victims, what they looked like, their names in some cases, and how he had killed them. Amirante had known Gacy for several years and the two were on the Norwood Park Street Lighting District, along with another northwest Chicago Democratic political luminary, Robert Martwick, Sr.

I've known Sam for years and when I hear him talk about the night of the confession—40 years later—you can sense the burden of what Gacy had unloaded on him. After that confession, he changed his tune. He did not testify at trial and, therefore, did not deny the crimes publicly at that time. The insanity defense he lodged was based upon an assumption that he had committed the crimes; the atrocity of the murders being Exhibit A that he was crazy. After the trial was over, Gacy thereafter took the position that he was innocent of all killings. Later he changed his story to include one exception: He had killed the first victim in self-defense.

During the time I knew him, Gacy's tired soliloquy was that he was innocent. He repeatedly referred to himself as the "34th victim." It was so ridiculous that whenever he started his pat responses about how he had no idea how those kids got to be under his house, I would just tune out.

As the execution loomed, I hoped that maybe, just maybe, Gacy would finally divulge something about why he did what he did. What would he have left to lose? Would such an unburdening help him when confronting his execution? Would it help the victims' families if only a little? Would it help me come to terms with something I could not understand? Or was his silence his last act of controlling outcomes? Even though the facts of his crimes had little to do with the nature of legal matters I was handling in his final appeals, I wanted desperately to break through his denials and get to the truth. Call it curiosity. Call it closure. Call it a reckoning. I wanted him to tell me why he killed those boys.

In late April 1994, I had an unusually long and stressful day. I had just finished a hotly contested and emotional hearing in a child custody matter involving allegations of physical abuse. The mother, my client, was convinced beyond any belief that her soon-to-be ex-husband was hitting their five-year-old son, pulling his hair, and spanking him. The father, a very presentable professional man who was tightly wound, adamantly denied the allegations and accused my client of conjuring up the accusations to gain an advantage in the divorce.

The judge was patently distressed by having to make such a difficult decision and ended up ruling that the father's visits would be supervised until an appointed child psychologist could speak with the child to get to the bottom of the issue. Although you are never convinced of the truth of any client's allegations or defenses, there is nothing good about a situation where a child is either a victim of abuse by one parent or the victim of alienating lies by the other. Even though I was just a lawyer in this drama, I felt the stress of knowing that either side's "truth" would adversely impact this child forever.

Minutes after returning to my office with the hope of relaxing, I heard the familiar robotic recording heralding a call from my imprisoned client. I braced myself. Gacy was an energy vampire. He could talk non-stop for hours and drain every last ounce of life from your body. He was a hollow husk of a human. There were so many lies, so many diversions, so many things he said and didn't mean—and later denied saying in the first place.

Once you understood that he was not integrated like a normal person, you understood that his lack of conscience allowed him to conduct himself in an amoral way with one goal in mind: To get exactly what he wanted. And that was usually to obfuscate and confuse the issues, redirect your attention away from the facts and the truth, and avoid addressing issues that did not reflect well on him. Gacy did this flawlessly because it was instinctive.

However, on this day after my child custody hearing, my already-eroded patience prompted me to think, "I am done with his bullshit." Today was the day I was determined not to let Gacy sidetrack me with his banter. I wanted something of substance out of him.

"Excuse me. JW. I hate to interrupt but I need a favor."

"Anything for you that don't entail me taking off these handcuffs, Dollface." A homosexual homicidal client was flirting with me about handcuffs. Charming.

"Okay." I breathed deeply. "If you did not kill them, how did those fucking boys and men end up under your house. How did they get there?"

A period of silence ensued, the length of which likely set a Gacy world record.

He repeated his standard line. "Ya know, the only thing I'm guilty of is running a cemetery without a license."

"Funny. I'll make sure that's on your gravestone, which, by the way, we have to get working on soon. John, if you aren't going to tell me, just use your imagination. Speculate. What could possibly explain why those boys were down there?"

"When you don't know the answer to a question, it's usually money," he said cryptically. (Pardon the pun about crypts.) "Money and information. Never give 'em away because you'll never get 'em back." Another Gacyism.

"Okay, and that means ...?"

"Snuff film operation." Gacy blurted out.

"What?"

"Snuff film operation. A snuff film is ..."

"I know what a snuff film is. I mean, I know of them. Uh..."

"At the time, there were lots of them films coming in from South America on the black market. Like from Panama."

"I think Panama is in Central America, John," I said in all my geographic correctness.

Gacy did not like criticism of any type. He was silent for several seconds, and I imagined him leaning against the wall at Menard giving the phone receiver the evil eye. Well, extra evil ...

"Someone," according to Gacy, was running a snuff film operation from his house without his knowledge. He was guilty of nothing and was as always the victim of his own generosity by allowing young men to live with him and provide them with gainful employment. In his backhanded way, he could have been telling me that he was the one running the business and that he was not just a crazed sexual predator, but a savvy entrepreneur who was profiting from these crimes. As if that made it more acceptable. While I will never know if any of this is true, I think this is as close to the truth as I ever got from him. Putting together everything I learned, here is the evidence that his Summerdale house was the home to a snuff film business:

Throughout Gacy's killing frenzy, two young men lived with him. In 1976, he picked up 18-year-old David Cram as he hitchhiked on Elston Avenue. Gacy offered him a job with his construction company, and Cram began work the same evening. Shortly thereafter, the boy moved into Gacy's house. The next day, in a benevolent house-warming gesture, Gacy tried to rape him. Cram moved out but continued to work for Gacy for two years.

Long before Cram moved in, a teenager by the name of Michael Rossi was described by his ex-wife Carol as "always hanging around." Both Cram and Rossi worked in exchange for money, drugs, and alcohol. Gacy told police after his arrest that he was having sex with both of them. The two testified at trial that they had dug the trenches in the crawlspace but denied knowing the purpose was to bury bodies.

Gacy told authorities that the two dug the trenches because he could not fit in the crawlspace. It is inconceivable that these young men did not know what Gacy was doing. If he was unable to access the crawlspace to dig the trenches due to his portliness, how could he drag 26 lifeless bodies into that space, layer them with lye, and bury them? He told authorities during his initial interrogation that he had accomplices and repeated this contention to several reporters during his incarceration.

Rossi and Cram were never charged. I believe it is likely that it was simpler to tag Gacy with all the crimes and more advantageous for the prosecution to win the world record for murder convictions against one person.

Rossi came from a powerful political family. It was reported that, during the police interrogation of Rossi after the Gacy arrest, his mother came to the police department and identified herself as the daughter of Vito Marzullo. Marzullo served as one of the most powerful aldermen in Chicago for decades. If it wasn't enough that Michael Rossi was the grandson of political royalty, his legal counsel, Ed Hanrahan, spoke volumes about the power his family possessed.

Hanrahan was one of the most prestigious attorneys in Chicago at the time, having served as the Cook County State's Attorney, the elected prosecutor of crimes in Chicago. Rossi, who had held menial jobs earning him just $5 per hour, could not possibly afford even one hour of this attorney's time. Interestingly, when I was hired 14 years after the trial, I called Rossi to see if he would be willing to shed some light on his role, if any, in the killings. Within about three minutes of leaving a message, Mr. Hanrahan returned the call, tersely telling us he was on retainer for Rossi and that there was nothing to talk about. Fourteen years is a long and expensive time to keep an extremely attentive high-priced lawyer at your beck and call, especially for a client who held mostly blue-collar jobs.

On another note, David Cram committed suicide in 2001 by hanging himself from a tree in a forest preserve.

Another fact pointing to other accomplices and possible filmmaking is the account of Jeff Rignall, a victim who escaped after a brutal episode of drugging, rape, and torture perpetrated by Gacy.

Rignall told police that there were occasions during his ordeal when he came to and saw another man in the room. That man participated in the abuse and performed oral sex on him. Given Rignall's description, many suspect the man may have been Michael Rossi. Rignall also said that he saw lights going on and off, meaning that there were others in the house, and perhaps a camera was being used to record the event.

There is no doubt in my mind that others were present during at least some of these crimes and that others could very well have perpetrated them.

Even if snuff films were not being made, there could have been a human trafficking ring in action. There were two other men that Gacy named as possibly being involved.

John David Norman was the ringleader in a notorious sex trafficking operation that supplied young boys to men across the nation. In a line of dozens of arrests for sexual crimes, Norman was taken in by Dallas, Texas police in 1973 after thousands of index cards were found at his home with names of men who allegedly paid for sex with boys.

Although Norman was never convicted of sex trafficking, he was later arrested and convicted of luring young boys into an apartment in a Chicago suburb, where he sexually assaulted them. Norman's closest associate upon entering Cook County jail, according to news accounts, was a man named Phil Paske.

Paske, who on three different occasions worked for Gacy and was friendly with David Cram, is alleged to have kidnapped Johnny Gosch, the first missing child to appear on a milk carton. Gacy talked to me often about Paske and Norman, referring to them as dangerous men and accusing them of "pimping" children for sex and making movies of the acts. When questioned about how he knew this information, Gacy feigned ignorance. The fact that he referred to the boys in the crawlspace as "bodies" rather than people is consistent with the way human traffickers refer to their "merchandise" in a detached, dehumanized manner.

Another little-known fact is that Gacy was out of town on the dates that several of the murders were committed. When he first made this contention to us, we thought it was his usual diversion-seeking bluster. But after taking a trip to the evidence warehouse in Chicago's lower west side where the crime scene evidence was stored, we found his meticulously maintained business records showing that he was, in fact, out of the state on the dates that at least several of the victims went missing. There were business receipts for motels and meals for the dates that substantiate his claims when compared to the prosecution's timeline. The receipts showed that he was in Pennsylvania and Michigan during these periods, which wasn't surprising because he had been hired by a drug store chain and ice cream franchise to build or remodel their facilities in many states, including those. Were others engaged in murdering victims during these out-of-town trips? Was his house used as a convenient burial ground for participants in a sick rape/murder club?

Finally, and I learned this much later: Police who searched the house following the arrest removed sophisticated movie camera equipment. Later, when the inventories were reviewed, the cameras did not appear on the list nor was the equipment ever recovered. Between this and the blackmail files, the resulting picture leaves me to wonder who might have known about Gacy's snuff films. There was no internet in the 1970s, and hardcore pornography and snuff films could have been a coveted commodity to the right perverted crowd.

Many believe that law enforcement looked the other way when Gacy was questioned about the disappearance of several boys who worked for him or were otherwise tied to him. The authorities seem to have given him break after break for no apparent reason.

Consider this: Gacy had a criminal conviction for sodomy in Iowa. In 1971, he was arrested when a teen claimed he had picked him up at the bus station and forced him to perform a sex act. The charges were dismissed.

In 1975 and 1976, two young boys who worked for him disappeared on separate occasions. That same year, police staked out Gacy's house when a nine-year-old boy went missing. Nothing came from it.

In 1977, Rignall escaped from his ordeal with Gacy and although charges were brought, they were dropped.

And later in 1977, a 19-year-old reported Gacy for kidnapping him at gunpoint and attempting to get him to submit to a sex act. Yet, he was never prosecuted.

After all these incidents, it staggers the mind that he kept getting a pass. Could it be the authorities were given the word not to bother this prominent, community-minded pedophile because of his connections? Were they unknowingly part of the cover-up? Did Gacy present such a solid front as a community-minded businessman and upstanding citizen that everyone was fooled? Or was he being protected by the people he refused to judge for their "sins and differences?"

When you look at the facts showing that he was not alone in these activities, the possibility of a snuff film or human trafficking operation is not far-fetched. He loved to kill, but he also loved to make money. He constantly bragged about his financial success and judged himself and others by how much money they earned. Even from the prison cell, John was interested in painting—not for pleasure—but for the money he could earn selling his "art" to keep his prison account flush.

On a visit to Menard, I brought up the snuff film theory Gacy had raised. I will never forget his response. He looked up at me, head cocked with those emotionless, expressionless, pale blue eyes and said, "Snuff film operation? I never said nothin' about that."

I immediately followed up. "John, if you can tell us about the involvement of Cram and Rossi and any of the others who may have been involved, maybe that would help your case or at least delay the execution."

"I'm not gonna do that," he said dismissively.

24.

WRITING ON THE WALL

I was in the office preparing for a deposition in a paying client matter and in the middle of outlining and shuffling exhibits, my secretary announced a call from Menard. She had accepted the charges and transferred the call.

Without thinking, I picked up the phone. "JW. What's happening?"

There was a pause and then I heard a familiar voice, but not one belonging to my condemned serial killing client.

"Hey, How ya doin'? This is Antoine."

"Antoine! What are you doing at Menard? Oh my God. What happened?"

I met Antoine Johnson just after I graduated from law school and moved to Chicago. Because my big firm was not giving me a feeling that I was "doing good" in the world, I signed up as a tutor with the Chicago Literacy Council, a great organization that teaches adults to read. Over 43 million adults—about 21% of the U.S. population—simply cannot read. The Council put its tutors through rigorous training on how to teach adults.

After completing my training, I was assigned to a 19-year-old young man named Antoine. Antoine's background was a wake-up call to me. Having been raised in a blue-collar suburb, I did not grow up in the lap of luxury, but we had food and clothing, and most of the children in my neighborhood came from two-parent homes.

We left our doors unlocked during the day, and everyone watched out for each other, especially the children. We walked and biked everywhere and as long as we returned home when the streetlights came on in the summer, our parents assumed we were playing sports and engaging in wholesome activities—and we were.

Antoine came from one of the most impoverished and dangerous areas in the city—Lawndale. In fact, Lawndale is one of the most dangerous neighborhoods in the country. In 1987, Lawndale had approximately 450 shootings and 80 murders. That is just one neighborhood. At the time Antoine lived there, unemployment was around 40%, and multiple gang shootings were a daily occurrence. Antoine dropped out of high school after he watched his mother's boyfriend stab her to death in their home.

Antoine's father, a paranoid schizophrenic, had also been murdered several years before. Antoine had been in and out of ten foster homes throughout his childhood due to his mother's drug problems. During his first year in high school, he split his time living in an unheated garage and his aunt's car. Despite this "homelife," he was on the track team and was one of the school's fastest runners. It is unclear why he had never learned to read in elementary school, but each year the teachers passed him into the next grade, probably thinking that holding him back would be worse for him and cause him to drop out of school. Or maybe they didn't notice he was illiterate.

In any event, after his mother's death, Antoine was told he would be heading back into foster care. Instead, he moved out of public housing and into a friend's apartment. That friend was a member of one of Chicago's worst street gangs. Soon, Antoine was running with the older gang bangers, carrying a gun, and shooting at rival gang members. It is common knowledge that veteran criminals use the younger ones to do their bidding, knowing that they would do less time if caught.

As I came to understand, he was not a leader; he was easily persuaded to commit crimes to please the father-figure gangsters who did not have his best interests in mind. Antoine was soon arrested and charged with gun possession and sentenced to five years in maximum security at Pontiac Correctional Center. One of the conditions for parole was that he make efforts to get his GED, which required him to seek help with his reading. The parole officer put him in touch with the Literacy Council, who put him in touch with me.

I met Antoine for the first time after work at a church basement in the South Loop, where I lived. He was a neatly dressed, African-American young man just over 6' tall and painfully skinny. His broad shoulders and narrow hips were those of an athlete, and you could see why he was such a good runner. As he entered the room, I noticed he held a newspaper and an imitation leather folio. I later learned that he held a newspaper while he was on the bus so people would think he could read. He had been pretending his whole life. Taped to the folio was a scrap of paper with the church address somebody had scrawled on it. How the heck did he find his way here on public transportation without being able to read?

For the next six months, I met with this shy young man twice a week and using the skills I learned in my literacy training, taught Antoine how to read. Even though he didn't know the letters of the alphabet, he swiftly learned them and the sounds they stood for. After he mastered the rather babyish books that were available for his reading level, I wrote stories for him about Michael Jordan and other sports figures, which Antoine read over and over with delight.

I took him to his very first sit-down restaurant where he nervously read and ordered from the menu. He was a polite, bright kid and was always respectful, on time, and appreciative. I can't imagine why no one had taken the time to help him. I found him a job at a fast-food restaurant that I knew hired ex-cons. He started seeing a girl from his neighborhood, whom he promptly impregnated.

After about six months, we stopped our sessions, and I lost track of him. In the last conversation I had with him, I told him to stay clean, keep reading, and take care of his baby. It turns out that, after we stopped communicating, Antoine lost his job, then his girlfriend. He became depressed and began self-medicating with crack cocaine and alcohol, using crime as a source of funding. He started running with the gangs again and during a robbery of a local business, was shot by the proprietor and came very close to dying. He was convicted of armed robbery and sentenced to 30 years. Thus, the call from Menard.

Word travels fast in prison, and almost everyone has a television. Antoine had seen that I was representing Gacy. He knew I had been down to visit Gacy and told me he wanted me to come and see him. He had no family and no friends and had not had a single visitor in all the years he was in jail. Although I was disappointed that Antoine was back in prison, it was not surprising given his upbringing, circumstances, and complete lack of support system.

With Antoine at Menard, I now had two buddies in that sewer. By the time I hung up the phone, I had promised to stop by and see him when I next visited Gacy—killing two jailbirds with one stone.

25.

FINAL EXCURSION TO DEATH ROW

Three weeks later, Greg and I were on the road for what would be our final visit to see Gacy at Menard. The plan was to drive down on Thursday, see Gacy for the entire day, and sleep over in scenic Chester, Illinois. The next day I would visit Antoine.

After our long, early morning trek, we arrived at the prison at 10:00 a.m. By the time we got through the red tape, it was 10:30 a.m. We were met with an agitated John Gacy who was as usual expecting us at 9:00 a.m. sharp. You never quite knew what you would get with him. His affect often belied what was really going on inside, or he was feigning agitation to get a reaction. Living on death row is tough on a person. I had done some research on the issue, and this helped me understand what might have really been going on to stoke Gacy's rage.

Psychological studies show living on death row is akin to torture. Living under such conditions would make a perfectly sane person crazy, and most people on death row have mental challenges to begin with. Psychologists have identified "Death Row Syndrome" as a mental disorder that inmates experience when they are put in isolation with an impending date with death.

According to some psychiatrists, the result of being confined to death row for an extended period of time in deplorable conditions, knowing one will die, can fuel delusions and suicidal tendencies in an individual. Half the inmates currently awaiting execution have been confined for at least 15 years; more than 200 have been incarcerated for more than three decades.

Prisoners awaiting execution live in cells half the size of a parking space. Many prisons, including Menard, are not air-conditioned and not properly heated. Menard inmates have died from both heat and hypothermia. Death row prisoners are isolated from others, most of them spending 22-23 hours a day in their cells. Due to security reasons, they are excluded from the normal activities to which other prisoners are entitled, which are not many. Also, consider how dangerous death row is. Your roommates are all convicted of killings that were so egregious they qualified for a death sentence. Plus, these men have nothing to lose. The suicide rate of death row inmates is ten times the suicide rate in the U.S. and about six times the rate in the general prison population.

It is no wonder that many condemned prisoners opt to commit state-assisted suicide by waiving their appeals. From the time that the death penalty was re-instituted in 1976 until roughly 2018, 145 prisoners have waived their appeals and asked that the execution be carried out. The most famous was Gary Gilmore, the subject of Norman Mailer's classic, *The Executioner's Song,* who was executed in Utah in 1977 by firing squad. His famous last words were, "Let's do it."

Note: Gilmore's plea for execution was the inspiration for the Nike slogan using those same words. The owner of the ad agency who devised the slogan in 1988 admitted that the murderous drifter was his muse. It takes the positive impact out of the swish, but just might make you run faster imagining a firing squad taking aim.

Death row inmates who seek to waive their appeals, known as "volunteers," must ask the courts for permission to go directly to the death chamber. Strangely, judges are very careful about giving such permission. To be "fair," some jurisdictions require a showing that the inmate is in fact competent to die. So many condemned defendants are depressed, psychotic, and mentally challenged that the courts are concerned executions for them will be unconstitutionally cruel and unusual as opposed to constitutionally cruel and unusual.

There is truly a bizarre set of legal concepts at work here. An inmate sentenced to death may not be executed while "insane," a condition construed as incompetent to understand the nature of the sentence and its implications. To do so would be contrary to the Eighth Amendment's ban on cruel and unusual punishment. It is also unconstitutional for an incompetent prisoner to make critical legal decisions, so an insane inmate does not have the competence to raise the issue of competence.

Another strange aspect of death penalty "volunteerism" is that outside parties almost always contest the inmate's right to waive appeals, bizarrely resulting in the criminal defendant fighting groups like the ACLU and Amnesty International.

In Illinois, there was the well-known case of Gwen Garcia. After serving time for smothering her 11-month-old baby, she murdered her abusive husband who had sold her into prostitution, and using a broken bottle to rape her, ripped a two-inch hole in her vaginal wall.

While most people fight for their life, Garcia fought for her death. She used all possible resources to hasten the execution. Meanwhile, activists from all over the world brought to public light her horrific childhood of being raped nonstop by two family members beginning at age six and being sold for $1,500 by her grandfather to an Iranian immigrant.

Organizations and individuals filed brief after brief advocating against Garcia's right to die including Bianca Jagger, wife of the Rolling Stone's Mick Jagger. Where was Dr. Kevorkian when she needed him?

Just hours before she was set to be only the second woman executed in recent history, Governor Jim Edgar issued his one and only commutation and ordered Garcia's sentence be converted to life in prison with the comment, "This is not the kind of case I had in mind when I voted as a legislator to restore the death penalty."

Ten years later while I was visiting a female inmate at Logan Correctional Center in central Illinois, I was introduced to Garcia who was quietly praying with several other prisoners.

It was hard to imagine she was responsible for the crimes I know she had committed, and it was likewise impossible to fathom the lifetime of abuse that led her to these actions.

...

Gacy was agitated during our last visit to Menard. I initially thought he was upset because he had less than a month left to live, but this was not the reason for his anger, as he expressed it to us. No. He was agitated because *The New Yorker* magazine had published an article which, rather than exalting his good character, made him out to be a psychopathic killer. *The New Yorker*? you are thinking. Not a publication you imagine is sitting around death row coffee tables to be picked up by your average mass murderer to chuckle at the clever cartoons or peruse the incomprehensible short stories.

About a month earlier, an author from *The New Yorker*, A.W., called us and pleaded with us to introduce him to Gacy so he could interview him for an "honest and positive story" humanizing him and his plight in fighting the death penalty. Of course, we did not believe he would ever write that kind of article. The only positive spin on the story would have to be published by Gacy himself, and his publishing days were fast approaching an end.

We initially declined to assist the author in facilitating the interview as it seemed that no one had anything to gain. But A.W. would not let up. Journalists cannot ethically pay for interviews. It would not be well received if readers knew that Gacy or his lawyers were being enriched by such a highfalutin' publication. A.W.'s urgings became more intense. He offered to come to Chicago and take us to fancy dinners (never happened) and even offered to have the world-famous, most highly paid photographer Richard Avedon, a frequent *New Yorker* contributor, take photos of us (also never happened). Finally, I told A.W. that I would mention the interview to my client.

Gacy was a contrary person. I told him A.W. wanted an interview, but that it was a bad idea. Of course, he said he was interested. With so little time left, I thought, he probably wanted a visitor. He asked me to immediately send him some articles that A.W. had written as well as his photograph, which I did.

Several days later, after receiving the materials, Gacy called me to say, "Get A.W. down here. When can he get here?" Ah, it hit me. A.W. was a very handsome man in a delicate, boyish way and was slight in build: Gacy's idea of something to do.

Within the week, *The New Yorker* journalist had flown from New York to St. Louis and made the trip to Menard. He met with Gacy over a couple of days, and both were mutually delighted with the experience. When the article came out a few weeks later, unsurprisingly, it was not at all sympathetic. From a literary standpoint, I thought the article was lacking in insight and did nothing to shed light on Gacy's conduct, his crimes, or the death penalty. It was too long, boring, and a rehash of everything else already said about the man. In the article, A.W. expressed disappointment that he did not take responsibility for his crimes, which was ridiculous. A simple reference to literature about sociopathic behavior should have told him this was part of the disorder. Gacy was likewise displeased.

As soon as we were let into the death row bullpen, Gacy greeted us without a handshake, his brow furrowed in anger. In one of his cuffed hands, he held *The New Yorker* open to the article. He wasn't bored with it. He was offended. In his normal, delusional way, he viewed himself as the victim of a bait and switch. Instead of praising his character and touting his innocence, A.W. confirmed that he was guilty. How could he? He spent the first hour of our visit alternating between blaming us for the introduction to A.W., criticizing parts of the article that he had highlighted and bragging about how he had the author in the palm of his hand. It was typical Gacy.

For the next several hours, we tried to corral his attention to focus on the important matters at hand: reviewing and approving briefs and petitions to be filed to save his life. He was very intelligent and understood the issues and arguments we were making. It dawned on me that Gacy had been litigating almost twice as long as I had been a lawyer, so no wonder he had a good grasp of the legal issues! As the visiting hours were winding down, he turned to me with an altered expression on his face, obviously wishing to change the subject.

His voice was softer, kinder, and almost paternal. "Now let's talk about your buddy, Antoine. He's quite the criminal."

Gacy had somehow gotten the scoop on my former student's rap sheet. Remarkably, he knew all about Antoine's prior conviction and the later one that landed him in Menard. Remember, there was no internet at the time, and even if there were, Gacy would not have had access to it. He was able to pay for intel from the outside world with money he earned selling artwork or with the currency he held as the country's most notorious criminal.

People seemed to be willing to do things for him because of his "importance" and the ability to brag that they had a relationship with John Wayne Gacy. In his book, *They Call Me Mr. Gacy* (not available on Amazon), he included numerous letters that were written to him asking for interviews, sex, and autographs. The one I recall most vividly was from a newbie television host asking him for an interview. Her name: Oprah Winfrey.

"So, you're gonna see Antoine tomorrow, I hear."

"Yes, John. The kid needs help."

"Well, listen. The kid was probably raised without a father as a lot of the n***s are in Chicago."

I bristled. "John, I really don't like that word."

Even back 27 years ago, before political correctness and before the mere utterance of that word caused loss of jobs and public shunning, I could not stand anyone using that word in my presence. Growing up in the not-so-tolerant suburb where I was raised, I remember a black postal worker being stoned in nearby Cicero while he was filling in for the usual mail carrier.

My parents adamantly prohibited the use of that word in our house, and my mother once forbade me from hanging around with a little girl in grade school whom she heard use the word in a jump rope game.

"Dollface, there are black n***s and white n***s and I don't treat 'em no different. Fact is, the blacks have an excuse 'cause they been discriminated against. Rather give 'em the benefit of the doubt."

Well, that's open minded of you, I thought. Aloud I said, "Antoine is a follower. He had no role model, no stable upbringing, and the gang became his family."

"Let me tell you this. That kid needed a father. Like my father. One who wouldn't let him get away with bullshit. Slap him around if necessary. Set an example of what it means to work hard and make him earn his keep. If he had that, he wouldn't be where he is."

So many layers of irony. Here is a world-record killer arguing that the man who relentlessly beat and berated him during his childhood was somehow good for his development, and had Antoine been fortunate enough to have a similarly-inclined father, he would have avoided jail.

Gacy continued, "If I were youse, I would tell him to get a prison job, put his money aside, and stay away from all those bad apples. He's young and skinny, just the way those predators like 'em. He's gonna be prime meat for one of those animals who don't have no morals. And he needs to join Bible study with the prison ministry. As a church-going Christian, I know God is the only one who looks after you."

Invoking a loose rendition of a Churchill quote, I said, "John, going to church doesn't make you a Christian any more than going to a garage makes you a car."

With that, we stood. Gacy wished me luck with Antoine and promised to have "his people" look out for him. We bade our goodbyes, knowing the next time we saw him, he would be closer to home and closer to the death chamber.

It was time to head to our motel on the outskirts of Chester.

•••

I have a liking for small-town America. I road-tripped with my family across most of the U.S. by the time I was ten and have fond memories of the indie motels and diners we frequented. What you see between big cities is, to me, the real America.

The river-town of Chester had a population of about 8,500 and was the Randolph County seat. It was home to more than its share of cheap motels and fast-food restaurants, all catering to the prison-visiting crowd. But Chester was best known for being the birthplace of Elzie Crisler Segar, the artist who created the Popeye cartoon character in 1929.

As we took a spin through the town, we came upon the recently opened Popeye's Hometown Shop and Museum situated in the town's old Opera House where Segar had worked as a film projector and performer starting at age 12. The cartoon character, Popeye the Sailor, who was best known for garnering strength from quick ingestion of canned spinach, later appeared in comic books, television cartoons, video games, and hundreds of advertisements for products ranging from spinach to candy cigarettes. In 1980, Robin Williams played Popeye in a Robert Altman-directed action movie.

We entered the museum and chatted with the proprietor while looking at original and reproduction comic strips, dolls, Pez dispensers, artwork, and framed advertisements. As we motored around the small town, we observed numerous murals and statues of Popeye, his girlfriend Olive Oyl, and other of his cartoon companions. I hear the Popeye Fan Club now holds a three-day event called Popeye's Picnic that includes many festivities including a Popeye Parade—in case you want to make the trip to Chester.

After browsing in one of the town's antique stores, which had more than its share of Popeye-related memorabilia, we decided to stop in and have a drink at one of the local watering holes. We spotted an old tavern in a building that was probably built in the mid-1800s. The letters on the faded sign were indecipherable, and the brickwork on the façade needed serious repair. Never one to judge a book by its cover especially when it comes to having a drink, I motioned for Greg and we ducked into the cool darkness of the narrow room.

After our eyes adjusted, we saw it was packed with locals wearing plaid, camouflage, and coveralls. Everyone was smoking. As we seated ourselves on the pleather bar stools, we saw the entire crowd turn to stare. "You're not from around here," their looks told us. The bartender, a 65-year-old guy with a wiry, gray head of hair and matching beard, came over and made small talk, asking us if we were in town for "The Prison or for Popeye?"

We answered simply, "Both." No one in that bar needed to know that we were in their town to try to rescue a murderous pedophile.

After finishing two rounds of the cheapest drinks since our college days, we exited the bar smelling of cigarette smoke and hungering for something substantial to eat. We found a diner just outside the city center, which served us an early and heavy dinner, and we were asleep by 9 p.m. at the Best Western.

...

The next morning was cool and sunny, a beautiful spring day. *Too bad we had to return to Menard,* I thought. We arrived just as visiting hours began. The guards were confused when we told them we were there to see Antoine. Visits for the general population were in a different part of the prison. It still took a long time for the guards to put us through their protocol and lead us to the visiting area.

Strangely, the visits in general population were conducted through a glass window, not face-to-face like on death row. You would think the prison would have looser security for the average killers and felons, as opposed to the worst of the worst. I sat down in my designated cubicle and waited for Antoine. As I looked around at the other inmates who had visitors, I noted that there was not a white face among them. Over 70% of Menard's population at any given time are minorities. About ten minutes later, Antoine arrived, handcuffed in prison orange, his hair cut short, his skin shining with sweat.

He smiled at me. "Hey, Snow. How ya doin'?"

I had forgotten that this inmate, too, had a nickname for

me. I always assumed it was because I am white, but who knows? The gangsta crowd is big on nicknames, and after having heard some of them, I could have done worse.

We talked for about an hour. We engaged in the usual prison conversation: How do you spend your day? How is the food? Who is your roomie? Have you had any trouble? How are your appeals going?

Antoine had a great memory when it came to me. He wanted to know if I was still with the law firm in the Amoco Building. (No.) Did I still live in the South Loop. (No.) Did I still have a cat. (Yes.) And was I still jogging. (Yes.)

I asked Antoine all about what happened and how he went back to his life of crime. He described his life as miserable. He had considered killing himself and said he was too scared to do it. When he was approached by his cousin's buddy who was in the Gangster Disciples to help sell drugs, Antoine thought it was a good career move or, more likely, his only career move.

He soon became addicted to crack and was living in and out of flop houses, abandoned buildings, and make-shift tents. The armed robbery was a logical conclusion to the story. The G. D. boss told Antoine to go into a small convenience store, pull out a gun, and demand cash. The gun he was given wasn't even loaded. But the store owner's gun was. He shot Antoine five times in the chest and stomach. It was a miracle he didn't die.

As Antoine described how he was in the hospital for two months following the crime, handcuffed to his hospital bed, he stood. Pulling up his shirt, he revealed a scar that started at his neck and disappeared below the elastic band of his pants, zigzagging like the Mississippi River down his skinny torso, ribs protruding among crudely drawn gang tattoos. Permanently etched upon Antoine's body was the story of his sad life.

During the long drive home, I thought, compared to Antoine, Gacy really hadn't been dealt a bad hand in life. Yes, his father was abusive, and yes, he was probably confused by his homosexuality. But thousands of children are born into similar homes with like circumstances. Gacy had the love of his mother and sisters. He was loved by two wives and four children. He had innate intelligence and the drive to succeed. He was a successful business owner who, in 2021 dollars, earned over $400,000 annually. The actions that landed him in prison were choices made. Whether he could control what he did, I am uncertain. But he had a chance.

26.

TEN MINUTES BEFORE THE EXECUTION
May 9, 1994
11:50 p.m.

Several minutes pass as Gacy sits up on the gurney looking straight ahead.

The guards nod to each other.

They place the leather straps over his protruding belly and concave chest. This is done carefully as the guards had rehearsed several days ago, with one volunteering to pose as Gacy. It's not often that one participates in an execution, so protocol must be followed. This is supposed to be a well-rehearsed death ritual.

But not so, as it would turn out ...

27.

ANOTHER DAY, ANOTHER ACCUSATION

About a month before the execution, I was home after an unusually easy day at work. It's hard to say that an eight-hour day is easy, but for a litigator that is a drop in the bucket. The blood sport of litigation is a hard way to make a living. Lawyers practice in areas other than litigation. They write wills and trusts (estate planning,) negotiate and paper business deals by drafting contracts, perform real estate closings, or work in governmental compliance. Those types of practices never attracted me because sitting behind a desk was not something that appealed to me.

Before I became a lawyer, I watched courtroom movies and television shows and was attracted to the drama and theatrics of humans fighting against the government and each other. I wanted to stand in a courtroom and be reckoned with. I wanted to use my brains to empower the underdog and to persuade the jury with a bit of theatrics thrown in.

Now, 35 years later, I must admit the life of a desk lawyer is more attractive than it used to be. Fighting in court is exhausting. Spending your entire day at odds with people when there is so much at stake takes its toll on the human psyche. Being professionally contrary and argumentative doesn't always sit right with me. Although I can do it and I think I do it well, I don't like the fact that my life as a litigator has seeped into my personal life. But that ship has sailed, and here I am.

Just a word to the readers who think they want to be courtroom lawyers: Spend a few months working for a litigation firm. You will either fall in love with it, counting the minutes until the bar exam allows you into the courthouse, or you will run the other way as fast as you can!

On this particular work night, I decided to watch the news, something I didn't do very often during the Gacy representation. Even though I was now on a first name basis with just about all of the reporters on local stations, I didn't want to hear about the execution. I was tired of seeing video replays of bodies being removed from Gacy's home in the 1970s. At this point in time, there was a lull in the legal maneuverings, and no issues were pending that were ripe for decision.

Expecting a Gacy reprieve, I was looking forward to some refreshing news—gun violence, gang wars, and political corruption—crimes that dominated and still dominate Chicago news. I turned on the local Fox station and saw my buddy, Walter Jacobson, at the news desk.

Walter was a legendary reporter in Chicago. In 1992, he had obtained one of the few jailhouse interviews with Gacy. During that interview, Walter had somehow convinced him to demonstrate how he performed the "rope trick," which was one of the devious ways he immobilized his victims before beginning the torture and murder phase of his crimes. Gacy seemed oblivious to how this kind of interview was not good for his ongoing appeals. As one of his lawyers said, "I'm not sure whether that interview was more about Walter's persuasive ability as a reporter or Gacy's delusion as a serial killer celebrity."

As I sat down with a glass of wine in one hand and the remote in the other, I thought about how it has been said that reporters begin the evening news with, "Good evening," and then proceed to tell you why it isn't. If it bleeds, it leads. I turned up the volume when I heard Walter say,

"Our top story tonight is about a 40-year-old unsolved triple murder case with a new twist. Could John Wayne Gacy, set to be executed in less than a month, be the killer in the 1955 Schuessler Peterson murders?"

Just when I thought it was safe to spend a Gacy-free night...

The historic Schuessler Peterson crimes were well-known in Chicago. On a Sunday in October 1955, three Chicago boys — Robert Peterson, 14; John Schuessler, 13; and his brother, Anton, 11 — made plans to venture downtown to see an afternoon movie. Peterson's mother helped them pick a Disney film, *The African Lion*.

They left for downtown and never returned. Hours later, the boys' parents reported them missing. Their fathers went to their intended destination and when they were not there, scoured other movie houses and locations the boys were known to visit. They were not found that day. Two days later, the boys' naked and mutilated bodies were discovered in a ditch on the north side of Chicago. It was disputed whether they had been sexually assaulted, but they had been held captive and were bound and gagged with tape. All three had been strangled, while Bobby Peterson had also been slashed across the head 14 times. The community was alarmed. This was at a time when doors were left unlocked, and parents allowed their kids to run free-range through the neighborhoods without serious safety concerns.

Anton Schuessler, Sr., was publicly heartbroken as he had lost his only two children. Shortly after the crime, he died tragically of a heart attack at the age of 43, which many thought was the result of his incredible loss.

As I watched the television segment, the three boys' smiling faces flashed on the screen followed by photos of the recovery of bodies. It seemed I just couldn't get away from this kind of thing. The news report included interviews with several investigators and people who had followed the crime for years. They posited a theory that Gacy was the perpetrator. The modus operandi was similar to that of Gacy, and the neighborhood where the boys lived was not that far from his childhood home.

A Chicago Police detective noted that the boys were seen in a building in the Chicago downtown area where Gacy was known to frequent later in his killing career. It was reputed to be a meeting place for gay men and prostitutes. Gacy had, perhaps, arranged to meet the boys there and had abducted them. The investigators told the reporter that they would like to question him about his possible involvement. His impending execution might put him in the mood to confess and thereby unburden his conscience before his demise.

I looked at the screen and said aloud, "You have to be kidding. To unburden a conscience, you first have to have one."

I did some quick math. Gacy would have been only 13 years old when these crimes were committed. How could he have overpowered three boys his age, strangled, slashed them, and somehow transported them to their resting place?

My gut said, "no way." I thought wryly, finally, Gacy is not guilty of something he is accused of. I had to talk to him about this. If by some slim chance he was involved or knew something about this crime from his associations with like-minded pedophiles, perhaps this information would be the currency necessary to buy him a stay of execution. Long shot, I know.

I arrived at the office the next morning, and, before taking off my jacket, I instructed my secretary to set up a prison call as soon as possible. I hadn't made it to my desk when Gacy beat me to the punch. By the look on my secretary's face, I could tell he was in a snit.

I picked up. "JW. How are you?"

"Those motherfuckers. They fucking think I killed the Schuessler Peterson boys? When I was 13 years old? I want you to sue those cocksuckers for defamation of character."

"Language, John," I said, thinking how ludicrous it would be to argue that this accusation damaged Gacy's otherwise pristine reputation. "John, you can understand why they are bringing this up now. Can't you?"

He was enraged. "I fucking didn't kill those kids. I was 13. I didn't have no car, and I ain't never been in that neighborhood. This is all just Walter Jacobson trying to make a name for himself by using the 'Gacy is a monster' thing."

He continued his ranting and raving for about five minutes until he tired himself out.

"Does this mean you don't have information for the police to stay your execution?" I had to ask.

Another three minutes of incensed protests ensued.

I thought Gacy might have been manipulative enough to feign knowledge about the crimes to buy himself some more time. It would also have given him an even broader forum to assert his massive self-importance. *Why be honest now, John?* I thought. But he wouldn't do it. End of story.

What about this accusation pissed him off so much? For 14 years, the gruesome details of his crimes were plastered all over the news, publicized in documentaries, made-for-television movies, and in thousands of books and articles. It was clear he enjoyed his reputation and took pride in his murders. Could it be that he considered the Schuessler Peterson murders as having been committed by an amateur and not worthy of his talents? Although that killer was not much of an amateur because here it was 40 years later and he hadn't been caught.

Interestingly, just a few months after the execution, the Schuessler Peterson crime was "solved," or at least someone was charged and convicted for it.

During an investigation into another cold case involving the killing of horses and the mysterious 1977 disappearance of the candy heiress and horsewoman Helen Vorhees Brach, investigators came across witnesses who implicated a man named Kenneth Hansen in these murders.

Prosecutors contended at trial that the three boys were hitchhiking when they were picked up by Hansen, 22 at the time. Hansen then took them to a stable where he worked. He sexually abused at least one of them and strangled them all. He was convicted based on the testimony of witnesses claiming Hansen had confessed to these crimes.

The next year, an appellate court overturned the conviction. He went on trial again in 2002 and after deliberating for approximately two hours, a jury once again found him guilty.

He was sentenced to 200 to 300 years in prison. Hansen's lawyers were adamant that Hansen had nothing to do with this crime and that another person had since confessed.

Due to the length of time between the crime and these trials, it was impossible for Hansen to present an alibi. Imagine trying to come up with an alibi after four decades have passed.

Hansen died in prison in 2007. While Kenneth Hansen may have been guilty of other wrongdoing in his past, and John Gacy certainly was, I highly doubt either one of them killed the Schuessler Peterson boys.

28.

WHY DOES IT TAKE SO LONG TO SAY SO LONG?

Justice is supposed to be swift, but in the case of a death row inmate, nothing is swift. From Gacy's arrest in 1978 until his death date was set in the Fall of 1993, 14 years had elapsed.

During that time, I had finished high school, completed a four-year college degree, attended law school for three years, and practiced law for six. Death row appeals plod along, and Gacy's were no different. The slowness is not because defense lawyers cause delays; it's because once a person is sentenced to death, numerous lines of appeals are available that are designed to test different aspects of the conviction. Those appeals were not created and upheld by liberal do-gooders; they exist because legislators and judges recognize that the Constitution guarantees a person's rights especially when death is the sentence. No matter what you think about people who are convicted, many are innocent, and once they go to their deaths, there are no "do-overs."

It may seem irrelevant to discuss actual innocence in a book about representing a guy with 33 victims, most buried under his house. But when you take on a death penalty case, you are not only advocating for the life of your client, you are championing for all who have received a death sentence and for those who might receive it in the future. The cause, at least in my view, was bigger than Gacy.

In Illinois, from the period of around 1994 to 2000, we

watched as one by one, largely black and brown men were released from death row based not upon technicalities, but actual proof that they were innocent.

By 2000, Illinois had executed 12 and exonerated 13 men sentenced to death. Hardly a confidence-boosting statistic. Only due to the aggressive defense given to death cases, we learned the many reasons why police, prosecutors, jurors, and appellate judges got it wrong and will continue to do so: coerced confessions, police torture, trial lawyers who are drunk, incompetent, and ill-prepared. Mistaken identity, rush to solve crimes, unreliable jailhouse snitches, unscrupulous and immoral law enforcement, and so many other factors contribute to this shocking statistic.

This caused Governor George Ryan, a Republican and life-long supporter of capital punishment, to issue a moratorium on the death penalty while he appointed a commission to study the issue and review all of the death row cases.

In 2003, Ryan issued a blanket commutation for all 167 inmates on death row, noting, "Our capital system is haunted by the demon of error, error in determining guilt, and error in determining who among the guilty deserves to die. Because of all of these reasons today, I am commuting the sentences of all death row inmates."

To this day, Ryan is seen as a villain by many who think the death penalty is the ultimate symbol of being "tough on crime" and the only appropriate means to deal with heinous murders. To others, he is an unlikely hero in the criminal justice system.

In one of the most notorious child murders in Illinois history, Rolando Cruz and Alejandro Hernandez were convicted of raping and murdering ten-year-old Jeanine Nicarico. In 1983, Jeanine was abducted from her suburban home when she was home from school sick with the flu. Despite no real evidence implicating the two, Cruz and Hernandez were convicted by 12 jurors and sentenced to death.

Shortly thereafter, a convicted serial killer Brian Dugan confessed to the crime with details only the perpetrator would know. Despite this, the prosecutors refused to drop charges.

The convictions were overturned on appeal, and they were again brought to trial. A new jury of 12 convicted the pair. Cruz was again sentenced to death. After DNA testing conclusively excluded these defendants, prosecutors did not relent. The appellate court again reversed the convictions. As a third trial was scheduled, it finally came to the attention of the prosecutors that there were lies and a mass cover-up of facts as reported by *The Chicago Reader*. A detective on the case quit his job because he said he didn't want to convict innocent people. A prosecutor quit for the same reason. But it was only after 12 years that one of the policemen went to court and disavowed the only remaining evidence—Roland Cruz's supposed account of an incriminating "vision."

After 12 years in jail, the defendants were released. Cruz was fully pardoned, and criminal charges were brought against law enforcement for their role in the wrongful conviction. In an interesting twist, Dugan was convicted and sentenced to death for the Nicarico murder, but due to Governor Ryan's moratorium and the abolition of the death penalty, he is now serving a life sentence. The same mistake that allowed Dugan to walk initially (wrongful convictions) saved his life in the end.

I met Rolando Cruz years later and could not help but marvel at the fact he had just barely escaped death by the government of a country I love with a justice system I respect. Thank goodness for the appellate process and the aggressive and persistent lawyers who volunteered to represent these young, poor minorities who were simply in the wrong place at the wrong time. These cases should make everyone question the accuracy of our conviction rates, especially when it comes to capital crimes. Crimes eligible for the death penalty—against children with multiple victims involving horrible rapes and torture—are most likely to result in guilty verdicts and death sentences, not always because of the weight of the evidence but because jurors are rightfully concerned about letting the accused person walk free. Horrible crimes can result in horrible decisions.

That was a long-winded way of explaining why the appeal process takes a long time even for Gacy, who didn't have any credible, actual innocence arguments or mitigating circumstances. The process was there for everyone, and Gacy's numerous lawyers took advantage of every one of them as they were required to do under our code of ethics.

By late April, we had a slew of court appearances and appellate court filings all of which resulted in immediate, stern, and sometimes scathing rejections.

Several courts issued their appellate decisions minutes after we filed our briefs, obviously not even bothering to read what we wrote. One court responded to arguments that we did not make but had guessed we would make. These judges not only made up their minds ahead of time, but they had made them up 14 years before when the name Gacy became a household word synonymous with evil.

If you think about it, what judge, elected or appointed, would risk her reputation, job, and personal safety to reverse a conviction for 33 murders? As I think back now, I see it clearly, but when I was in the middle of the circus, it was hard for me to understand why our appeals were not treated at least with some semblance of respect.

Bad clients and bad facts make bad law, and we were making some bad law.

29.

EXECUTION DAY
May 10, 1994. 12:02 a.m.

It's now time for the event to happen. The moment so many have waited for.

The gurney is propped up. Two guards enter the chamber with rubber gloves, ready for action.

Gacy's arm is swabbed with alcohol for no apparent reason, infections being of concern only to the living.

"John Wayne Gacy, do you have any final words?"

For once, he is speechless. Why would he give the world any further professions of innocence that wouldn't be believed? In his mind, he is the victim.

The dirty, straw-colored curtains before him are opened by some unknown force. On the other side of the glass is another small room with two dozen simple folding chairs, all of them occupied. The show is beginning for those in the audience who were lucky enough to have won a lottery that allowed them to be present. With so many families hoping to get closure for their horrendous losses, there is no way to accommodate all the people who want to witness this event.

The audience faces the window, trying to get a good look at the once uncontrollable psychopath who is now strapped down and subdued: the person who had destroyed their lives.

Sitting in the front row is the man who prosecuted Gacy 14 years ago. With his *Guinness Book* record of murder convictions still intact, the lawyer is the only one in the room with a slight smile on his face, pleased that he is finally able to watch his legal handiwork come to fruition.

Gacy doesn't bother to look at his audience. He would not give them the satisfaction. Not that this was going to give satisfaction to any of them. If they came to see Gacy tortured and tormented, they will be sorely disappointed. Ironically, the horrifically vicious acts he committed during his life were supposed to guarantee him a relatively painless, predictable, and dignified death. Compared to the end of the 33 lives he took, this was a walk in the park.

One surgically-gloved guard unbuttons Gacy's prison-issue shirt and places a heart monitor on his chest. It is important to know when the deed is done. The guard carefully rebuttons his shirt, making sure it is straightened for the big moment. The other guard takes a needle out of a case and lifts Gacy's forearm. He inserts the needle into a vein, allowing an innocuous saline drip to pave the way for the trio of death cocktails that are waiting on deck.

Gacy looks straight ahead with unseeing eyes. There is no way to read what is going through his mind during these last moments. Is he saddened his life is ending? Does he regret choosing the momentary pleasure of killing over being allowed to live out his natural life? Is he frightened about the prospect of his perceived afterlife? Or is he relieved the demons that urged him to commit such disgusting and vile acts would finally be silenced?

The guard behind him nods and then hits one of the buttons on the death machine. The lead-off drug, sodium thiopental, is released into Gacy's arm. This anesthetic agent will normally render a person unconscious in less than 30 seconds. It is efficient, effective, and alone can cause death. On cue, his eyes close and the tension he held in his body suddenly releases. His entire being appears to collapse slightly onto his resting place. His chin dips.

One down, two to go. The machine continues to hum for several minutes. On the other side of the glass, the witnesses rustle anxiously in their seats, unsure how to react to this bizarre ritual before them. The hum stops, and there is a slight click. The second drug, pancuronium bromide, automatically begins its way into Gacy's arm, its purpose to relax the muscles to prevent flailing and unsightly spasms that might be difficult for viewers. Because the drug relaxes the muscles that allow breathing, it too can cause death.

This is where the carefully planned execution veers off course.

It is suddenly obvious that the line is clogged and the chemical inside has stalled en route to its deadly destination, rejecting Gacy's body as if it knew what evil lay within. The reason for the malfunction is simple chemistry. The first two lethal injection chemicals, when combined, frequently cause the intravenous line to clog. No medical professional is there to rectify the situation; doctors are prohibited by the Hippocratic Oath from participating in the causing of harm.

There is confusion and chaos among the execution crew. Someone finally has the presence of mind to end the show. The curtains close quickly with a whoosh.

The witnesses, their eyebrows knitted in confusion, turn their heads right and left, murmuring to their fellow lottery winners, "What the heck is going on …?"

30.

FIGHT OR FLIGHT

Right around the time of these legal setbacks and in the spring of 1994, I started to experience serious anxiety. I was having trouble eating—not something that ever happened to me before or since. I couldn't sleep, and my body ached. At first, I didn't attribute my condition to Gacy. I can handle stress extremely well. I have always been one to take on way too much, care too much about the outcome, and try to cram in as much as I possibly can each day. Even when I decide it's time to play, I plan it ambitiously and then execute with gusto.

I did not immediately identify stress as the culprit. Most people don't. It's hard for a person under serious stress to be self-reflective. Science shows that a stressed person's nervous system goes into "fight or flight" response, generating adrenaline and other hormones. Muscles tense in anticipation of assault. The body shifts its energy resources toward fighting off a life threat or fleeing from an enemy.

In the case of representing Gacy, there was truly a life threat, that being the State of Illinois, the hundreds of prosecutors assigned to deflect our legal missives, 30 plus judges at all levels ready to reject everything and anything we filed, and 90% of the people in the country who, even if they were anti-death penalty, wanted Gacy dead. Trying to save a life is not a routine job for a lawyer, and I had never been tasked to do so. The fact that doctors and first responders encounter life or death situations on a daily basis makes me glad I am an ambulance chaser and not a driver of one!

After finally ruling out all other causes for my unprecedented lack of appetite and other symptoms, I diagnosed myself with an acute case of execution-itis, with no available medicine or cure. Had I thought there was a chance of winning anything for Gacy, it might not have been as stressful. Working hard toward a goal with the possibility of some success is not stressful to me. However, it is heavily taxing to work like a dog knowing that no matter what you will soon be dragged to the pound and put down.

Does the fact that I felt so much anxiety about Gacy's death mean I liked him, that he was my friend? For three decades, people have asked me this question. It's hard to answer. If I had met him at a party or on the bus, I probably would have thought he was funny and gregarious, but also braggy, a little too full of himself, and a bullshitter. No different than many narcissistic know-it-alls who run for political office.

We would not have formed a friendship because I didn't have a whole lot in common with him, my hobbies being comparatively benign. Also, he wasn't a whole person with all the normal dimensions. He was an empty shell you could not wrap your emotions around. However, when you are thrown together with someone with a common purpose (staying alive) you form a bond that is unlike any other I have ever had. It wasn't about liking him; it was about not wanting him dead. Even when he fought with me about strategy and did things clearly against his best interests, I could not hate him. I wanted to help him. I wanted to save him ... from himself.

Despite the hoopla and the bizarreness of the circumstances and heinous actions that Gacy committed, the simple fact was that the life of a human being was in my control. I realized I could not alter the hand I was dealt. The facts were what they were. I did not want him to die. Was this stressful? Other than suffering the death or illness of loved ones, I cannot name a more stressful period in my life.

It was about this time that I realized others around me were also upset by the impending execution—people who were not thrilled with my representing him initially.

Greg's 14-year-old son, Rik, who lived with us, was at first annoyed when his high school classmates thought his dad's involvement with a serial killer was cool. As time went on, Rik would talk to Gacy on the phone when we weren't home, and he developed an oddly warm relationship with the man. Gacy had given Rik advice on how to "fit in" and told him not to worry about his sexuality. Rik had no girlfriends up to that point, so we did not know his sexual orientation. It was Gacy in whom Rik confided that he was straight.

Gacy's response? Either way, it was okay. After Gacy reported this news to us, Greg and I had a sit-down with Rik and told him that talking to a murderous sex offender about these issues might not be a good idea. Merely allowing this client to call our house with a teenaged boy living there was a child welfare issue in and of itself. The fact is that Rik had taken a liking to Gacy and was extremely upset that a human being with whom he had made a connection was going to be executed.

My 70-year-old father was also living with us, while he was going through some health challenges. At first, my father, an avid supporter of capital punishment, was against our representing Gacy, warning me about ruining my reputation. He had no desire to be associated with this man and certainly did not want his daughter to be. Over the months, he, too, had spent time chatting with Gacy when he called the house. He soon became very upset by his impending death, saying to me several times, "I guess he isn't hurting anyone now. What's the use in killing him?"

It's different when you come to know someone. Instead of thinking: *Why keep this guy alive?* You think: *Why kill him?*

Even my office staff who had collectively cringed when they found out about our infamous client became agitated and upset, often questioning whether the execution was going to happen on May 10 and what our chances were of at least getting a stay.

Gacy called daily and chatted it up with my secretary, paralegal, and associate. He remembered birthdays and sent

Christmas cards and laughed about what was funny in the world. It's hard to describe the transformation that occurred over the months, but it's fair to say that to those who got to know him, Gacy was a human being who was not entitled to walk freely in the world but who should have been able to continue to live and breathe until death came to him the good old-fashioned way.

After the execution, I began teaching a course on the death penalty. As an exercise, I would assign each student an Illinois death row inmate. The students would study the trial transcripts and appellate briefs and talk to the inmate's attorney. They were free to correspond with the defendant, visit him, or work on his appeal.

As part of the final paper and presentation, I asked the students to conclude if justice dictated whether the inmate should live or die. In all the years I taught the course, 100% of the students—even those who were adamantly in favor of the death penalty—believed their inmate should live. It didn't matter if there were issues of actual innocence, whether the inmate was likable, or whether the crimes were particularly egregious.

My takeaway: When you know the condemned personally and experience their humanity, the death penalty at least for that person simply is not tolerable.

31.

GALLOWS HUMOR

Humor has always been an important part of my life. It has gotten me through many hard times, difficult relationships, and stressful situations. My sense of humor derives from both nature and nurture. My father was a stand-up comic for over 50 years and, therefore, not only do I have some of that humor embedded in my DNA, I grew up with a parent who was funny all the time … always looking for the funny angle in life and encouraging me to do the same. Since I was very young, I have been a student of comedy. I am fascinated by what makes a joke funny and why certain people have the ability to make others laugh.

People ask me all the time what Gacy was really like, which is one of the reasons I finally wrote this book. I would be omitting a huge part of the answer to this question if I did not tell you this: John Wayne Gacy was funny.

I can hear my critics saying, "You think killing 33 boys is funny, Karen?" No, I do not think that John Wayne Gacy's horrors are anything other than serious, tragic, and disgusting.

But if you ask me what Gacy's prevailing personality traits were, I would have to identify his sense of humor as one of them. It amazed me that a person who was so damaged, so evil, and so unlikable and dark in many ways, possessed a sense of humor when it was contrary to everything else about him.

Analyzing humor is a lot like dissecting a frog, goes the old joke: No one laughs, and the frog dies. Sigmund Freud had a theory that people often tell jokes as a kind of relief system from anxiety. One famous study showed that humor can leave the comedian with a feeling of control over a situation that would otherwise cause them to feel powerless. Other studies show that people with a great sense of humor, particularly those who enjoy dark humor, have higher IQs than their less-funny peers. And let's not forget that almost all of us find a sense of humor to be an attractive quality that makes a funny person more desirable to be around.

I believe that humor often comes from a place of darkness, ala John Belushi, Chris Farley, Henny Youngman, Richard Pryor, and Robin Williams. It is no news that many of the world's funniest people suffered from anxiety, depression, and addiction. Gacy fit into pretty much all of the above categories, and perhaps his use of humor was a way of masking the sociopathic and homicidal part of him—much like his dressing up as a clown.

Given all of this, how did Gacy make me laugh and what caused him to be funny?

During one of my visits, I mentioned that I had seen a television talk show where women were interviewed about falling in love with notorious inmates. One woman claimed she had an ongoing penpal relationship with him. She professed her love for Gacy and told the host that he had proposed to her.

"What's up with that, John? Playing for both teams without telling me?"

He looked me straight in the eye and said, "Oh, that's bullshit, Dollface. You're talkin' about Sue Terry. She has a bunch of kids. Three of them are in the penitentiary... Like I'm going to marry into a family like that!"

As you can see, he used his infamy as a serial killer in a self-effacing way that made the jokes unexpected and funnier than they would otherwise be. Even though you are never prepared to laugh at a joke told by a man who had no regard for decency or human life, you found yourself laughing despite it all.

Gacy told jokes constantly, and he told them well. Many of his jokes were dirty and sexual, and some of them were just plain silly. When I complimented him on his joke-telling in one of our phone calls, he told me, "Serial killer jokes are funny as long as they are properly executed." He also told me that he had consoled the wife of one of his serial killer friends by saying, "At least he died doing what he loved."

My father and Gacy would often talk on the phone, telling each other joke after joke. It was truly bizarre. One day, I came home to the sound of my father chattering away and laughing on the phone with Gacy. I realized they were discussing his last meal before his impending execution.

My father: "John, what are you going to request for your last meal? It should be fresh strawberries ... Do you know why?"

Pause.

"They're out of season."

Gacy repeated that joke to anyone who would listen, and when the time came, he included fresh strawberries in his last meal request. Was it humor or homage that made him do that? We will never know, but I do know that the State of Illinois would have sent an agent on a plane to California for fresh strawberries if necessary to assure the execution proceeded as scheduled.

John Gacy was a big practical joker before his stay at the "Menard Hilton." However, he had nothing on me because I consider myself to be the master at practical jokes and especially surprise parties. So, here's the story about how John Gacy and I played the ultimate practical joke. After his death.

When I met Greg, he complained to me that because he came from such a large family, no one remembered his birthday. Like a dog with a bone, I took that woe-is-me complaint and turned it into a ten-year history of elaborate surprise parties, some of which made national news.

On one occasion, I had Greg "arrested" by a Chicago Police officer and brought to "court" where he was tried and convicted of all kinds of wrongdoing before 100 friends with a real prosecutor, defense lawyer, and judge.

One year I arranged for an ambulance to arrive with lights flashing. A uniformed EMT put Greg on a stretcher and brought him to a medical clinic that I had rented out (for a charitable donation) where celebrants were dressed in scrubs to witness the roasting of Greg via medical diagnoses. We served Gangrene Salad, Mammogram Chicken breasts, and Vasectomy Potatoes.

In an election year, I rented out a huge hotel ballroom where I threw a campaign rally for Greg running for President on the "Surprise Party Ticket." His friends and a Bill Clinton impersonator gave campaign endorsements for the feted Greg.

And the list goes on.

Gacy had read about these parties and constantly wanted to know how I planned them and managed to surprise Greg over and over again. I don't know if it was the humor or the deception that captivated him, but it was a constant topic of conversation.

About two weeks before the execution, Gacy and I were chatting on the phone. Out of the blue, he blurted out, "You know, Karen. I'm coming to Greg's birthday party this year."

Note the timeline: This was April. Gacy was scheduled to die in May. Greg's birthday was in October.

"John," I said, "there is a snowball's chance you will be alive in October, let alone free from jail ... and invited!"

"That's cold, Karen. You wouldn't invite your favorite client?"

"Don't get your tux out of storage, JW."

"Seriously, Dollface. I wanna be there. I will be there in spirit." And so was hatched the Gacy/Conti practical joke of the century.

It was decided that I would take out my mini-recorder, and Gacy would record a birthday message for Greg. If the State of Illinois had its druthers and the execution occurred on May 10, I would wait until the morning of Greg's birthday and put the message on his voicemail so he would receive the ultimate surprise: Birthday wishes from a serial killer who had been dead for five months. Macabre, yes ...

32.

GROWING A KILLER

There is a black and white photograph of an eight-year-old John Gacy saved on my computer. He is standing near his childhood home in Chicago, dressed in a double-breasted suit. His brows are furrowed, and his eyes squint against the sun. His mouth is set in a straight line. His jaw seemingly clenched. His crew-cut hair has been combed smoothly across his head, maybe by his mother.

He appears uncomfortable as boys often are when they are dressed in formal clothes against their will. Was he going to church? A family party? I search his features, harshly lit by the sun. I wonder: Had the combination of this child's internal wiring and early external trauma already begun to twist his psyche? Had the abnormalities begun to surface yet, the ones that later caused lives to be stolen and others to be destroyed for generations? Was this boy's innate innocence gone by the time someone propped him in front of this camera? When was the point of no return?

I think of young John as a small tree, a sapling, perfectly formed and destined for a straight and healthy existence. With proper light and water, the tree should have grown straight and strong. But early on, the branches were bent by the weight of his family's dysfunction and perhaps a deficiency in their cellular makeup. Despite the deformities, the branches continued to grow in their malformed state, becoming strong in their defective and contorted character until the tree was fully formed, seemingly solid but irretrievably twisted.

Gacy was born and raised at 4505 Marmora, a bungalow in the Portage Park neighborhood on Chicago's northwest side. Marmora is an Italian word for "marble," which is derived from a Greek word meaning to flash, sparkle, and gleam. Nothing about Gacy's bungalow gleamed; it was solid and squat in its typical brick makeup.

For over 100 years, Chicago bungalows, which had close ties to the Arts and Crafts movement, have been an iconic part of the city's residential architecture. In the early 20th century, when Americans wanted to own homes, especially those who had immigrated here from foreign lands, the style was perfect to accommodate growing families and the narrow residential city lots. More than 80,000 bungalows still stand today, many having been expanded over the years with dormers, front and back porches, and other additions.

When Gacy told me that he had grown up in a bungalow, I asked him to describe it. Amazingly, it was my childhood home to a tee: the dark red brick façade, the front steps leading up to the left, and the layout of the room configurations. His bedroom, like mine, was upstairs.

After the execution, I drove to the house on Marmora. It was as if my own Berwyn bungalow had been lifted by a Kansas twister and jettisoned 10 miles due north onto the property. It's strange to think the events that transpired in a home identical to mine likely caused such epic evil.

Gacy was born on March 17—St. Patrick's Day—1942, the second child of Marion and John Stanley Gacy. His father was an auto repair machinist and World War I veteran. His mother was a homemaker. Gacy had two sisters, Joanne, who was older, and Karen, a few years younger. After her brother was arrested, Joanne never spoke to him again and stayed out of the public light.

During my representation, I got to know Karen Kuzma. We have maintained a sporadic but warm email relationship over the years. I sometimes hesitate to contact her even just to say hello, knowing that I am a reminder of the end of John's life. But I feel an odd bond with her. I think of us as the "Karen bookends" of Gacy's existence: Karen K. being there at the very beginning and Karen C. being there at the very end.

Karen is intelligent, kind, and honest. She is horribly affected by Gacy's acts, the pain of the victims' families and her own family, and the loss of her only brother at the hands of the State 30 years ago. Although she has come to terms with what happened, she is forever haunted by what Gacy did and puzzled at the reasons for his actions. At the same time, she adored her only brother and mourns his loss daily.

For months following the execution, Karen didn't sleep for more than an hour at a time without awakening in tears. In my view, she is a victim of Gacy in a different way than the murdered victims' families. The difference is that she gets no sympathy and no opportunity to be righteous in her grief. Much of what I will tell you about Gacy's upbringing is from my conversations with Karen.

Gacy's parents were practicing Catholics. John Senior was an "extremely strict" parent. His father had died when he was ten and had no "father to learn from." There was swift and sure punishment if any of the children violated the rules. He used a razor strop to spank all of the children, and the violence was also visited upon his wife.

Young Gacy, however, got the brunt of it. He could never live up to his father's masculine expectations and demands. His father's anger became worse when he drank to excess in the family basement, which led psychiatrists to speculate that Gacy's penchant for using his crawlspace as a burial ground was related to his father's subterranean rants.

Despite this corporal punishment and disapproval, his sister claims, "My father did not create John's killer side." Gacy confirmed that in conversations I had with him. He waffled between showing respect and admiration for his father's discipline and hard-working lifestyle and referring to him as a "sonofabitch" whom he could never please.

Gacy's mother was a kind but passive woman, a good, nurturing parent, and homemaker. The dynamic of a hard-working, hard-drinking father and stay-at-home mother who minded the home and her husband's mandates was fairly typical of the 1940s and 50s and by itself wasn't the catalyst of their child's maladies.

Gacy was "just a normal kid." Despite his parents naming him after the western actor, John Wayne, the epitome of masculinity, he did not live up to his moniker. He wasn't tall or muscular and wasn't particularly interested in or talented at sports or traditional boyhood activities. According to Karen Kuzma, her brother loved to cook, bake, and garden. I spoke to Gacy many times about these activities. He talked frequently about recipes and the "right way" to cook or season a dish. We had many talks about my adventures as a novice gardener in Oak Park. I told him the story about how I once planted 200 tulips without thinking to read anything about the right way to do it. It turned out that I had planted them upside down. It was an inside joke between us, and he would sometimes start a conversation by saying, "Hey, Dollface, how are those tulips doing in China?"

Ever the know-it-all, he gave me frequent and good advice about how to plant, divide, and fertilize my hostas and pachysandra. Every time I take out my shovel, I think of Gacy, for reasons relating to gardening and not burying bodies.

Throughout his childhood, Gacy was frequently ill and suffered blackouts. Head injuries have been closely tied to violent behavior. Criminology studies show that a large percentage of inmates had suffered serious head injuries before committing their crimes. About 8.5 percent of U.S. non-incarcerated adults have a history of traumatic brain injury (TBI). In prisons, approximately 60 percent have suffered at least one TBI.

Richard Ramirez, "The Night Stalker," suffered a serious head injury when a dresser fell on him, necessitating 30 stitches. He was also knocked out by a swing in the park, which caused him to suffer from epileptic seizures into his teens.

David Berkowitz, "Son of Sam," suffered two head injuries at a young age, including a car accident.

Henry Lee Lucas, "The Highway Stalker," and Dennis Rader, "The BTK Killer," likewise sustained head injuries.

A fascinating study by criminologist Dr. Adrian Raine showed that serial killers have lower activity in the pre-frontal area of the brain. This is the area that controls aggression, concentration, and impulse control. Psychopaths were also found to have a shrunken amygdala—the part of the brain that controls emotion. This might explain their lack of remorse or guilt.

Karen tells me that at age 13 her brother started a job as a delivery boy for their local IGA grocery store. He rode his bike to deliver groceries on Saturdays and holidays when he was out of school. A year into his job, while making a delivery to a second-floor apartment, Gacy slipped and fell down two flights of icy stairs, hitting his head several times. He passed out, was taken to the hospital, and missed work for a week.

Then, at age 16, while he was walking across a school playground, someone pushed a swing that hit him squarely in the head, causing him to pass out. The doctor kept him overnight in the hospital for observation, and he suffered headaches for weeks afterward. In fact, he suffered headaches well into adulthood, but we do not know if they were related to this incident.

Karen notes that her brother suffered "blackouts" and "epileptic seizures" for many years. "Some were real, and some could have been fake." She recalls that, when Gacy was 19 or 20, doctors treated him for a "blood clot leading to his brain." At some point, the spells stopped and "the doctor said the clot was dissolved."

Most psychologists and criminologists agree that Gacy's upbringing was far too unremarkable to explain his criminal conduct. On the other hand, what childhood history could explain it? Although early on, he was discovered to have hoarded his mother's underwear and on occasion worn it, he displayed none of the traditional early warning signs that a serial killer was in the making: bed-wetting, fire-setting, and animal torture. Karen reports that the family had two dogs that Gacy treated gently and kindly.

Besides physical trauma and his father's abuse, the issue of sexual abuse is thought to be important in explaining Gacy's later conduct, although that is not to say that people who are sexually molested turn out to be serial killers.

During his post-arrest mental examinations, he revealed two sexual incidents. The first occurred when he was just five. While accompanying his mother on a visit to a neighbor, the 15-year-old daughter of that neighbor took Gacy into her bedroom and began to fondle him. When their mothers discovered their children together, the girl's mother slapped the girl in Gacy's presence.

Three years later, when he was eight years old, he was fondled and assaulted on several occasions by a male contractor in his mid-30s. The builder, who had a casual friendship with Gacy's father, would take the boy out for ice cream and then show him "wrestling holds," which involved Gacy's face being shoved into the man's crotch. After a few of these incidents, young Gacy told his father that he didn't want to be alone with the contractor and their contact ended.

Psychiatrist Dr. Saul Rappaport, who spent 65 hours interviewing Gacy, believed the trauma of his father's abuse was at the core of his dysfunction. It was "the forerunner for the relationship he had with his victims." Gacy handcuffed victims, telling them of the torture he would inflict, which made them beg for their lives. This recreated his feeling of helplessness at his father's hands. At that point, he would become his father and punish them for begging, a demonstration of their weakness.

He taunted the boys as homosexuals, whether they were or not, accusing them of wanting to have sex with him for money or otherwise. He projected his own feelings of inadequacy onto his victims, who were mostly small in stature like him.

I have heard the recording of Gacy being questioned by the police shortly after his arrest. When the police referred to the bodies under his house, he blurted out, "They're just a bunch of homosexuals." It was almost as if he were saying, "So what? Why should their existence matter?" Remember, many of the victims were not homosexual, but Gacy thought of them as such, probably so that he could dehumanize them summarily.

If there is anyone who knew John Gacy, it was his sister, Karen. She has agonized for years trying to identify what caused this turn in him. She has many stories of his protective behavior toward her as a child and teenager, his kindness to the elderly and his neighbors. She talks of her brother's generosity in helping people he knew and people he didn't. Was this a ploy to cover his dark side with good acts?

Karen thinks the "trouble started" when Gacy moved to Iowa. Even though he was married and had two children, something his father finally approved of, he began to associate with a sexually adventurous crowd that wife-swapped and engaged in group sex. They were prominent members of the community who had a common interest in this type of behavior. Karen seems to think this conduct was the cause of his later aberrations, and after his incarceration in Iowa for sodomy, the purpose of murdering victims was simply to leave no witnesses.

Soon after his arrest, Gacy called his sister. She asked him directly, "John, did you do these crimes?" He answered yes. That confession was the only reason she would have ever believed her brother was guilty. Karen thinks her brother truly had two people inside of him. One was hard-working and kind, and the other was wholly lacking in morality and conscience. Until his arrest, she simply never knew the latter person existed.

33.

DEATH DAY

May 10 is a day that is permanently etched on my mental calendar. After seven months of toiling away on Gacy's legal work, that day was literally the deadline—the day my client would either live or die.

As I look back, it was both an end of a beginning and the beginning of an end. It was the day that would end my relationship with a human being whose life I was trying to save. It would begin a chapter in my life that included the permanent association with an executed serial killer, something that forever changed the course of my life.

The morning began early for me as I sat in my kitchen with a cup of strong coffee in my hand, watching the sun rise over my suburban lawn. It was an unlikely day for an execution. It was gloriously sunny and crisp. For the first time that year, I noticed the intense spring colors—the deep green of the wet grass; the red and yellow tulips proudly guarding the fence line while the pink peonies bent with the weight of the morning dew.

Squirrels leaped from budding branch to branch, hoping to find their breakfast. All of nature's creations were busy striving to stay alive, straining to live another day. The drive to survive is natural, I thought. The drive to kill is not.

I was already exhausted. Greg and I had been up since 3 a.m. putting the final touches on our last legal briefs that would be filed in federal court and then the U.S. Supreme Court, requesting a stay of execution—a temporary halt to the wheels of the juggernaut of capital punishment. It promised to be a long day as the execution was set for midnight. Executions are traditionally done deep into the night as if the scheduled taking of another's life must wait until darkness puts its shroud over the whole process.

Caffeine aside, I was particularly agitated that morning. Maybe judges, prosecutors, and governors were accustomed to these life-or-death legal maneuvers, but I wasn't. This was my first death penalty rodeo, and I was frightened. I was fearful our efforts would fail, although I knew they would. I was also afraid for Gacy even if he didn't have the sense to be afraid for himself. Perhaps, I was most apprehensive of what would happen if we did get a stay. Would the process start all over again, with another death date set, putting us into an execution day limbo? Prolonging the inevitable?

As I prepared for the day, I remember thinking: How does one dress for an execution? "My Dress for Success" manual would not help me here. A classic black silk suit with a white knit top. Simple gold necklace. A lawyer attending a funeral, I thought. I was scheduled to be interviewed at my home via video feed on *Good Morning America*. From there, we would go to the prison to meet Gacy and await word from the courts. I needed to be strong. I needed to put aside my emotions. I needed to be a spokesperson for someone whom no one wanted alive. I needed to say my goodbyes.

The camera guys from the network arrived at my house just as I put the finishing touches on my makeup. They set up in the living room while I got them water and coffee. I was to be interviewed at the top of the show by host Joan Lunden, a journalist whom I have always respected.

As I sat down, I was mic'd up and dusted with powder. Shortly afterward, I was connected with New York for the preshow audio/visual testing. As I learned through my involvement with the media, television is driven by the visual, not necessarily the audio. To this day, when my friends and family see me on television, they can never recall what I said, but they can describe in detail what I wore and how my hair was styled. For television interviews, it is crucial that you look good. Your hair must be smooth, and your face cannot be shiny as that can make you look sweaty and nervous. Solid colors are preferable. In a live piece, the interviewer has draconian time deadlines, and your answers must be short and impactful.

As I sat in my living, room, I went over my talking points:

1. I was representing Gacy because of my opposition to the death penalty, not because I thought he should be released from jail.

2. The death penalty is wrong, even for someone as evil as Gacy.

3. I understand how the victims' families want this man dead, and my heart goes out to them.

4. Every defendant deserves an aggressive defense, and I am simply doing my job as part of the best criminal justice system in the world.

The audio came on. The ABC producer greeted me and told me for the first time that I would be on the same screen with the parents of Robert Piest, Gacy's last victim. The Piests had been particularly vocal about wanting Gacy executed. Rightly so. Gacy took Piest from a local drugstore while his mother waited outside to bring him home to celebrate her birthday. His body was tossed like trash in a nearby river. It was impossible not to tear up whenever they talked about the son they would never see grow up.

In a split second, I made a decision. I told the producer I was not going to appear simultaneously with the Piests. My client killed their beautiful boy 14 years ago. I would not argue with them about what should happen to his murderer. If I were in their shoes, I would want him dead and doubt I would have been as dignified as they were throughout this process. My job was to advocate for my client, which I would do until he stopped breathing, but I would not lend myself to this display of distress.

I took off my microphone and told the producer I was not doing the interview. The producer anxiously asked if I would wait.

One minute later, Joan Lunden came on the screen during a break. I told her that while I understood that heartbreak and anger make good television, I could not and would not be part of it. To my surprise, she immediately agreed that this was wrong. There were two separate parts of the story and two separate storytellers. Relieved, I sat back down. I gave my interview and the Piests gave theirs. It was the one thing I felt good about all day.

With the camera crew gone, Greg and I got in the car and headed to Stateville Correctional Center in Joliet, Illinois— about 45 miles southwest of Chicago—where Gacy was to be executed. He had been flown to the prison from Menard before morning. Our mood was tense and the conversation minimal. I turned on the radio to distract us, and, as I flipped from station to station, I was bombarded by news reports on the impending execution.

At one point, Greg turned to me and asked how I was doing. I was so far into myself I didn't know how to answer. There was nothing in my experience that could prepare me for this. As a lawyer, I try hard not to let emotions into my legal work, but the looming specter of my client's death caused feelings of intense angst, fear, and desperation.

As we approached the prison, we saw that cars had started to line the road, and people were setting up camp to await the big event. Stateville is an all-male maximum-security prison. Like Menard, the building is old, opened in 1925. It sits on 2,200 acres of land and boasts 33-foot walls with surrounding guard towers. Stateville housed over 2,000 inmates and was one of three sites in which executions were carried out in Illinois.

Gacy was the most notorious prisoner that ever graced the halls of this fine institution, but he was in good company. Richard Speck, who raped and killed eight nursing students in their Chicago dormitory in 1966 called Stateville his home for 25 years. Earlier, in the 1920s, two wealthy University of Chicago students, Leopold and Loeb, were locked up in Stateville after they kidnapped and murdered 14-year-old Bobby Franks for the sole purpose of committing the "perfect murder."

Loeb was represented by none other than Clarence Darrow, who was reportedly paid $1 million for his legal services—over $15 million in today's dollars. A separate facility nearby, Joliet Correctional Center, was used in *The Blues Brothers* and today is a popular attraction for people interested in Chicago history, early prison life, and deviant criminals.

As we drove through the entrance and approached the prison, we noticed large tents set up for the massive media congregation. How nice of the prison to welcome the big show that was about to unfold. I was surprised no signs were heralding "Welcome to the Execution of the Killer Clown." It was like a morbid Cirque du Soleil. Up to this time, there was no criminal story in the Chicago area that had received this much attention, and I am not sure if there has been since.

As we entered the building, the guards, seeming to know who we were, ushered us in. We checked in and went through security. The officers spent an inordinate amount of time asking about "medical contraband" and checking our bags, pockets, and exposed orifices for pills, aspirin, allergy medicine, cough medicine, and even vitamins. Those in power in the Land of Lincoln wanted to avoid the embarrassment of Gacy executing himself prematurely with the help of Dr. Kevorkian-like attorneys. There will only be one killer in this process, thank you.

We were led down the usual set of dingy hallways. The odor of disinfectant, human sweat, and decay emanated from every nook and cranny. After what seemed like an hour, we were finally let into an area containing a row of unoccupied jail cells. Gacy was sitting at a small wooden table on the outside of the cells, shackled. On the table were his files and what appeared to be a small Bible. Neither seemed to be of much use to him at this point. Several guards hovered around the perimeter of the elongated room watching us warily. Gacy rose and greeted us with a grand gesture to his spacious surroundings, "I'm moving up in the world, huh?"

We grabbed folding chairs and sat down. The comb marks in Gacy's white hair made defined streaks in straight lines from front to back, giving him the appearance of having freshly showered. I wondered if showers are provided for the condemned on the day of execution.

His blue shirt was neatly pressed as usual and his face, normally sallow and waxlike, was flush with excitement. This was a big day for him. After 14 years of monotony at Menard, he was in a completely different venue from his usual confines, although this one was also filled with cells, bars, and guards.

He excitedly told us about his flight from Menard by helicopter at dawn the morning before. He was thrilled to be outside and flying high. He described the cornfields and landmarks he saw from the air and said he wished it would have lasted longer. He was proud to tell me that the Director of the Department of Corrections accompanied him on the helicopter and had treated him like "royalty" until Gacy turned and said, "Nic, when you fly on a plane, do you realize that every part in it was supplied by the lowest bidder?"

He had a joke for everything. Normally, I would laugh along with him, but today it was just so hard to find anything amusing.

Despite my ill temper, Gacy was effusive about the visitors he would have that day and about his last supper. He loved being the center of attention and asked us expectantly if he was getting "a lot of good press," a narcissist to the end. If the State of Illinois thought that Execution Day would be a hard one for this man, they were mistaken. At least at this point, he was acting like it was the best day of his life.

Our visit was more than just a social one. We had a serious legal matter to attend to immediately. We needed to make sure he was in his right mind. There is legal precedent that prohibits a person from being executed if he is not sane at the time. It is unconstitutional to execute someone who can't understand their impending demise. If the person fails to have mental competency, lawyers can ask for a stay of execution until that person is properly medicated or recovered enough to understand the situation. Although this is the law, the standard is pretty low.

Case in point: Ricky Ray Rector was a death row inmate in Arkansas. He was very badly brain-damaged due to a self-inflicted shot to his head that had destroyed his frontal lobe. On the day of his execution, after being served the pecan pie he requested for his last supper, he insisted on putting it aside because he was saving it "for later." He was executed as scheduled with the blessing of Governor Bill Clinton, pie left uneaten in his cell.

We had previously informed Gacy about our need to perform this wellness check. Part of me thought that when the day came, he would try to fake insanity or lack of awareness to buy more time. When we began asking him test questions to make sure he was okay, he simply brushed us off and told us that he was "as right as rain" and he wasn't going to "argue no insanity defense again." Once was enough and "look where it got me!"

Once again, Gacy had it under control. Under the law, the man who killed 33 was perfectly sane and ready to be executed.

34.

LAST CALL

Once we determined that Gacy was healthy enough to be injected with poison, we decided to leave the prison to allow him to meet with his friends and family who were waiting to say their goodbyes. We would return later in the evening with news about the appeals and, in all likelihood, to say our final goodbyes. I motioned to the guards to let us out, and as one of them called for assistance on his police radio, Gacy stood up and said to him, all wiseguy, "You're letting them out? Not fair. You never take me anywhere …"

The guard looked at him, glanced at us as if to ask if it was ok to laugh, and shook his head. The other guards turned away. Nobody likes an execution. Despite Gacy's penchant for extinguishing human life, no normal person wants any part of what's effectively state-sponsored killing.

Exiting from the jail into the warm May sunshine, we were reminded that there were many hours left in this day, but that Gacy would never live to see another one. We were confronted by hordes of reporters and cameramen. They were yelling questions at us … "How is he taking it? Is he waiving his appeals? What is he having for his last supper? Is he finally showing remorse?"

I could never understand how cameramen walk backward in a crowd, but there were at least 40 of them doing just that as we moved toward the parking lot. As we arrived at the car, one of the overly aggressive local television anchors blocked me from getting in the passenger door.

He demanded, "What do I have to do to talk to Gacy?"

"Ask me tomorrow," I said reaching around to open the door. He repeated that on the news that evening. Not my finest hour.

We slammed the doors shut and they locked. "Now where?" Greg and I asked at the same time. As we drove down the road toward the main route away from the prison, we noticed even more celebrants lining up for the execution. This was a Monday! Why weren't these people working? Like a storm cloud on the horizon, this crowd was growing restless and seemingly hostile.

We were ravenous, and with time to kill (pardon the pun) we decided to go to a quiet restaurant on the quaint main street of nearby Lockport. There was a Mexican restaurant that we often frequented when we went to court in Will County or on one of our prison visits in nearby Joliet. It was our treat after what was usually a not-so-pleasant experience. By the time we got there, it was about 2 p.m., and the lunch crowd had dispersed.

The dimly lit restaurant was decorated in the bold colors of Mexico. The tiled floors shone immaculately, and the colorful "papel picados" banners strung across the ceiling reminded us that this was our very own Day of the Dead. Our waiter came over to say hello and take our order. I am usually not a lunchtime drinker. When I started practicing law at a large firm in Chicago, the old-timers still took their lunches with at least two martinis. I can hold my own when it comes to alcohol, but I could never drink like that at lunch; that is to say without ending up asleep under my desk within 30 minutes upon returning to the office. On this occasion, I preempted the joint decision-making process and blurted out, "Dos margaritas en las rocas, sin sal." Greg looked at me with renewed respect and nodded. A good decision, his expression seemed to say.

When the drinks arrived in their heavy blue glazed glasses, we lifted them and recited our standard criminal defense lawyer toast.

"To life," said Greg.

"Without the possibility of parole ..." I replied.

So, there we were in the middle of a beautiful spring afternoon in a little town drinking a margarita while our serial killer client held court in one of the nastiest prisons in the country, thinking that it was the best thing that ever happened to him. At this point, it was a fait accompli. All our briefs were submitted. Somewhere, appellate judges were ignoring our arguments, issuing opinions denying Gacy any reprieve, and feeling relieved that they would not be forced to disappoint the public's cry for this litigant's death.

We were well into our fajitas when the restaurant door clanged, admitting six reporters and two cameramen. I had no idea how they found us. Knowing they would not leave until we gave them a statement of some sort, Greg and I stood up and met them near the door.

For the next hour, we gave each reporter a short interview, explaining the status of the appeals, Gacy's mental well-being, and the timeline for the execution. When we finished the interviews, we promised the journalists we would talk to them later that evening and returned to pay our bill.

As we were signing the check, our waiter, who had figured out what the hubbub was about, looked at us and said, "*Es un mal hombre, eh?*"

We returned to our car and headed back to the prison. This time the route was completely jammed with cars and bystanders. The execution was still six hours away. The lawn resembled a Super Bowl media mob scene. There were vans and trucks and satellite dishes.

The reporter from Rome with whom we had developed a relationship blew kisses to us from a rental camera truck. Dressed in black from head to toe, she was playing the part of serial killer widow.

Other local reporters ran up to our car, microphones extended, impeding our way to the parking lot. I saw television call letters that were obviously from different states. Reporters were darting around trying to decide how to get the best shot of the prison and interviewing themselves for lack of anything better to do.

We passed through security again, and as we were led to the waiting room, one of them told me that the Illinois Attorney General's office had staffed a prison conference room down the hall with 30 assistants. They were armed with computers and telephones, poised to fend off any last-minute appeals. The State was not going to take any chance that my client would escape tonight's scheduled festivities.

Upon entering the room, I found Gacy surrounded by a group of visitors. He was chatting nonstop, animated, and smiling. I looked over to the side of the room and saw what people had been talking about and anticipating for months: the last supper.

Despite the State's inhospitable efforts to execute this man, they sure showed hospitality in providing the condemned man with a feast to behold. The tables along the cracked and peeling wall held a veritable buffet. We take food for granted, and, even if we don't always indulge in our cravings, we know that if we want a Big Mac, a lobster tail, or a Snickers bar, we can easily get it. But for prisoners, their denial of good food over the years is a constant source of conversation, almost an obsession.

Gacy, who liked to eat, was positively euphoric. Apparently, the food had been delivered a while ago; Gacy had eaten, then rested, and then had eaten again. The door to the room opened again, and several lawyers who had represented Gacy entered. Seeing that my client was otherwise occupied, I went over to check out the buffet table more closely.

On May 10, 1994, dinner at Chez Stateville included several buckets of Kentucky Fried Chicken (original recipe,) deep-fried shrimp, french fries, a pound of strawberries, (fresh as requested) and of course Diet Coke. As I was taking in the sight and smells of these culinary delights, Gacy peeked his head around the throng of visitors and yelled over to me, "Hey Dollface, gotchya some Diet Coke. Help yourself."

I yelled back, "Wow, JW. This is some spread." I thought,

You'd better watch your cholesterol. I don't want to have to resuscitate you.

Let me remind you how creepy it was that Gacy had ordered KFC for his last meal. Before his Chicago killing spree started, he had managed three KFC franchises in Waterloo, Iowa. Not only did he maintain the secret recipe for chicken there, but he lived a secret life abusing boys and in particular, one of his employees, which landed him in prison. Now that Gacy's date for kicking the bucket was here, he was eating his last meal from one.

Greg went over and said hello to the group of lawyers who had congregated around Gacy. They immediately began talking about the status, viability, and timing of outstanding appeals.

Gacy, who could not be bothered with this line of conversation, motioned for me to sit down next to him to talk. His face was flushed, and he appeared to be happy. He was animated and chatty, asking me to describe the scene outside of the prison, what reporters were there, and what they were asking us. He was thrilled that the execution was getting this much attention and appeared enthused about all of the goings-on. He had no questions about the status of his appeals and seemed unaware that he was going to die in just a few hours. His good cheer made it easier for me to handle the situation, although I realize now that it was probably a coping mechanism. An inveterate liar and denier of reality, he had better tools than most to handle these final hours.

A steady stream of visitors entered the waiting room. I recognized some as Gacy family members and long-time friends, but many I had never seen before. I learned later that some were penpals and others were his neighbors from Norwood Park. I was stunned that these people who hadn't lived near him for 14 years and whose property values had probably plummeted when his crimes were exposed, showed genuine fondness for him, seemingly disregarding the deeds that put him in this room. This was the strangest part of the entire experience. This man was loved by others. Unconditionally. It is hard to fathom how they could have true affection for someone so evil, but I guess you could ask me the same question: How did you get along with Gacy for all these months knowing what atrocities he had committed? How could you care about him and his fate? It took me many years to answer those questions.

He was a human being. As a member of the human race, there was a connection, no matter how tenuous and no matter the circumstances. Despite his inhumane acts, when you experience that connection personally, you feel the profound wrongness of extinguishing that life. It's easy to say, "Kill him," but hard to sort through the complex emotions of that reality.

While visitors came and went, we chatted with everyone politely, trying to hide our anxiety. It was like a prison cocktail party without the cocktails, although in a few hours there would be one strong one served to the man of honor.

Just after 7 p.m., the guards summoned us to take a call outside the waiting room. We stepped out and were led to a room with a telephone. As expected, it was our co-counsel advising us that the U.S. Supreme Court had voted 8-1 to deny a request for a stay of execution. Justice Harry Blackmun, a death penalty opponent, was the lone dissenter. Gacy's 14-year odyssey through the appellate courts had come unceremoniously to an end.

Greg turned to me and asked, "Which one of us is going to tell John?" I knew he wanted me to be the bearer of bad news. This wasn't because Greg lacked the courage; it was because he knew Gacy would take it better coming from me.

I said, "I got this."

We returned to the room and Gacy was standing next to his chair receiving goodbye hugs from several older well-wishers. Several had tears streaming down their faces. I hated to interrupt, but, as his lawyer, I had the duty to give him the news. I walked over and addressed his visitors.

"Excuse me, may I have a word with John?"

Gacy stared daggers at me as if to say, "What now?"

I pulled my client away from the circle of visitors and put

my hand on his shoulder.

"JW. We just got word from the Supremes. Not good."

His eyes were furtively scanning the room. He appeared not to hear me.

I squeezed his shoulder. "John, are you listening? This is it. The appeals are over. We lost. This is going to happen tonight."

He finally looked at me. His affect was flat. His eyes had taken on a grayish hue, the color of an abandoned file cabinet. "Did they give a reason?"

"No. But Justice Blackmun dissented. You have one fan."

He smiled. He grabbed my hands with his handcuffed ones. "Make sure that when I'm gone, you send him a thank you note from me."

And with that, my condemned client returned to the business of socializing.

35.

TO DIE A LITTLE

With our job completed, I felt we had little reason to stay. Gacy was fully engaged with his friends and family, and it seemed our presence in the room was detracting from his ability to enjoy his final hours. He was overjoyed to be surrounded by loved ones and permitted to touch them and walk about freely—something he was forbidden from doing for 14 years. We were nothing but a reminder of the failed efforts to stop what was to come.

Greg and I walked over to him, parting the crowd, and I whispered in his ear, "Do you need us here, John?"

Imminent death did not stop his smart-aleck streak. He quipped, "Not at your hourly rate."

I couldn't let Gacy get the last word. "We can still send you a bill, you know ... Death does not excuse non-payment of lawyer's fees."

He loved it. "Naw, I don't need youse guys. I'm all good."

Greg said, "Well, John, in that case we're going to say our goodbyes."

He snapped to attention. Even though he was a sociopath with no true emotion, he knew very well what social custom required, and he was going to do what was expected.

He turned to us. "Well, let me have a minute with youse, but I wanna talk to you separately." He gave me a theatrical wink. Nodding at Greg, "You first, big guy."

Gacy pulled Greg over to the side of the room and they huddled together talking softly for two long minutes while I waited my turn. What could they possibly be saying? How do I say goodbye to someone who has a scheduled time of death? When you know someone is going to be intentionally killed, your instinct is to call the authorities. But, in this case, it was the authorities who were doing the killing.

Suddenly, they straightened up, and Greg threw his arms around Gacy in a huge bear hug. As they parted, Gacy patted Greg on the arm with his cuffed hands as if to comfort him. Greg's eyes were brimming with tears.

"I'll wait for you outside."

On deck, I approached.

"Well, John, I just want to say ..." My throat closed and I couldn't speak.

"Listen, Dollface, this is really important. You can't forget to play that joke on Greg—you have to remember to put my birthday message on his voicemail in October."

I welcomed the diversion. "I won't forget, JW. It's going to freak him out."

He chuckled. "I'm never gonna die. Mark my words."

"The State seems to have other plans, John."

"Well, I just wanna tell ya something that you ain't gonna like to hear. But you're gonna be glad you represented me. Your career's gonna skyrocket. And your obituary is gonna read: 'Karen Conti. Represented serial killer John Wayne Gacy.' You're gonna be forever connected with me."

My killer client, hours away from execution, was giving me a career pep talk. Before I could react, he leaned into me and put his hands up around my shoulders—a death row hug of sorts. I hugged him and he held on to me for what felt like a full minute. For the last time, I smelled that combination of cheap cologne, hair tonic, and sweat.

He whispered in my ear, "I want to thank you for everything you done for me. I mean it. I appreciate it. I love ya."

My head was full of mixed emotions. I know he couldn't mean those words, so would it hurt me so much to return the sentiment to a dying man I would never see again?

"I love you, too, John, and I am so sorry we didn't win this for you."

"You did your best."

We separated. "Thank you, John. I hope it all goes okay. I'll be thinking of you."

"You take care of yourself, Dollface."

With that, Gacy turned back to his throng of friends and family, and I turned and beelined to the door, not wanting to break down in that room.

An author once said, "To say goodbye is to die a little."

As the waiting room door shut behind me, I knew that in about four hours, Gacy was going to be more than a little dead.

36.

EXITING THE EXECUTION

We again exited the prison and were met with the sight of hundreds of media trucks from around the world with throngs of reporters trying to pull us in for interviews. We managed to move through the mob to our car parked in the special guest area. I was numb and shaking from the emotions of the day, lack of sleep, and disbelief that this was going to happen. The State was going to kill my client.

Driving off the Stateville campus, the scene was bizarre and chilling. Hundreds (looked like thousands to me) lined the streets leading away from the prison for at least two miles.

The very vocal crowd resembled what one witness described as a "boozy carnival" with a splash of rock concert anticipation. The smell of marijuana wafted through the cool night air, and even with the car windows closed, there was the stink of skunk. Many were drinking from beer cans that they were extracting from coolers nestled in beat-up pickup trucks and hitched pulls.

The age range ran the gamut with some older celebrants certainly old enough to remember the news stories of Gacy's arrest and some born well after he was incarcerated. There were infants and grade-schoolers throughout the crowd. Apparently, many parents believed this was a good chance for a family outing, even though it was late in the evening and a school night. Always good to teach your kids about right and wrong. Would they live to tell their children about this historic night?

There were drums beating, music blaring, and people dressed in clown suits. Some wore garish face makeup. How long did they plan these gruesome costumes? Were they left over from Halloween? The signs were varied and creative. *Ding Dong the Clown is Dead, An Eye for an Eye,* and *No Tears for the Clown*.

But the one that caught my eye was *Execute Conti!* It was printed neatly in blue block letters on a whiteboard; somebody took the time to do it right. Interesting how you can pick out your name easily no matter where it's printed. There was also the anti-death penalty contingent among the crowd holding signs like, *Wrong, Even for Gacy* and *Death Doesn't Justify Death.*

These observers were the quiet ones, perhaps because they believed this should be a somber occasion, but more likely because they feared retribution from the righteous revelers. I noted that someone had anticipated the crowd's needs and had placed several Porta-Potties along the way for the convenience of those heeding the call of nature. No need to strain kidneys while someone is being executed.

As I drove down the narrow road away from my soon-to-be-dead client, it slowly dawned on me that this was a dangerous crowd. Despite the raucous cheers and imbibing, this group could turn very ugly very quickly. I knew with conviction that if we were spotted and recognized in our car, it would be a matter of only a few minutes before this mob would pound on windows, break into the car, and up-end it with us inside.

While I have always had intense sympathy for the victims' families and understood how they could personally hate me enough to harm me, I thought: *Even they could not be enjoying this eerie demonstration.*

If the State is going to use its awesome power to take the life of a human being, doesn't this process deserve some dignity and decorum? It is no wonder that these crowds were not given much media attention. Even the most sensational reporters knew that this celebration was unseemly and a poor reflection of our baser instincts.

37.

**EXECUTION DAY
May 10, 1994
12:16 a.m.**

The clogged line cannot deliver the muscle relaxant, the second dose of the hat trick of lethal injection chemicals. Although such a glitch was predicted by experts, it seems all the rehearsals are for naught.

Nobody knows what to do to finish off our condemned man who looks to be sleeping peacefully on the gurney in contrast to the desperate and frantic participants in this ceremony.

We don't know exactly what is happening to Gacy as the team struggles for over 40 minutes to unclog the machine. They try to reattach the drip and fail. They check to see if he has succumbed to the first drug even though he did not receive the second two. No such luck. They need to make this work.

Meanwhile, Gacy is unconscious. Or is he? Doctors will later speculate that he was in agony but unable to move as he was slowly being asphyxiated. In short, he was being suffocated to death. It was as if the death gods were inflicting upon Gacy a taste of his own evil medicine.

Finally, the line is unclogged. The second chemical is released. The relaxant streams into his body. The machine hums. There is another click, and the clean-up chemical, potassium chloride, is finally allowed to flow into his already-collapsed form, stopping his heart from beating, and putting an end to his existence on this Earth.

At age 52 years and 54 days, John Wayne Gacy is dead.

The curtains open again, the death crew having almost forgotten the expectant crowd waiting on the other side of the glass.

The heart monitor is checked, and the time of death is announced at exactly 12:58 a.m.

38.

THE NIGHT OF THE EXECUTION:
May 10, 1994
1:35 a.m.

Fifty miles north, my law partner and I sit in a restaurant bar in Chicago's Greektown, watching the television coverage of my formerly alive client. The owner had thoughtfully kept his business open for us while we waited almost one hour for Gacy's death to be broadcast. Or maybe the restaurateur was fascinated by the news coverage and did not want to miss how it all ended.

I was overwhelmed with exhaustion, both from the day's events and those of the past seven months during which I, a young, inexperienced lawyer, handled the highest-profile case in the country.

I had exerted all possible efforts to save the life of the world's most successful killer and was hugely unsuccessful. The ending was certainly expected. What was not expected was the profound feeling of loss. I spent seven months talking to, eating meals with, and fighting for a living, breathing human being. And despite the horrors and misery he had wrought, I felt a connection to him.

My purpose here is not to tell you Gacy should not have been executed. Everyone has an opinion on capital punishment, and nothing I say will change your mind one way or another. My purpose is not to make you feel sorry for a serial killer because what you know of this man is only his heinous acts. No, this is a story about how I formed a relationship with another human being, how that relationship was congenial, contentious, fascinating, and at times humorous. My story is about how that relationship surprised me and changed me forever.

I once heard it said that there is no such thing as justice. Justice is simply an idea that makes people feel better. There is only revenge or mercy, and you can't have them both. My story is also about how I learned how true this is …

39.

NIGHTMARE ON THE MISSISSIPPI

After representing Gacy, I started having nightmares. They continue to this day and repeat over and over. They are not about Gacy himself as one would expect. He has never come to me in my dreams. When I knew him, nothing was scary about him, and I was able to compartmentalize his crimes.

The recurring nightmare is about Robert Piest, that handsome, 15-year-old boy who was the last victim, the reason Gacy was finally caught. The story of Robert is haunting.

On December 11, 1978, Robert's mother, Elizabeth, drove to the Nisson Pharmacy in Des Plaines to pick up her son who worked there part-time. It was her 46th birthday, and the family planned to celebrate together.

Elizabeth was told that Robert was applying for a job with a man who was promising construction work paying $5 per hour, double what he was earning.

It was Elizabeth Piest's birthday and she would never see her son again.

Within the hour, Gacy brought Robert to his home and began torturing him. Not long after, he was killed and then dispensed to the freezing Des Plaines River. Over the years, I read accounts of the heartbreak his parents had suffered and how they had kept his bedroom intact as if by doing so he would come back to their home.

My nightmare: Robert Piest appears before me sporting

1970s feathered hair from the yearbook photo that appeared in the press repeatedly, his likeness forever frozen, both in age and fashion.

He is walking frantically around a modern-day drug store looking for a scrap of paper he had dropped. I keep trying to help him, and he won't take it.

He runs to the front of the store and then to the back, and I chase him. He is gone. I run through the storage room, out the rear door, and down a dark, wooded road. The slick road twists downhill and ends abruptly at the edge of a river.

I know that this is the Des Plaines River, which eventually wends its way to the great Mississippi. Gacy dumped at least four bodies here. I jump in the water. The current takes me down, down, down. As I become exhausted and feel I am about to succumb to the force of the water, I awaken in my dream, but not in reality.

My mind sees what I know is Robert Piest's empty bedroom, his twin bed neatly made, Cubs memorabilia on the wall, high school banners hung over his desk, which is scattered with notebooks, tickets, and boyhood keepsakes. A museum preserving the memory of a dead boy. The door slams shut behind me, and I cannot get out. And then I wake up.

I feel as if I know Robert Piest. I think I will run into him someplace where I least expect it and have a conversation with him. He is almost exactly my age. When I see him, he is tall and I suspect he's successful and has a family of his own. What would I say to you, Rob? May I call you that? Would I thank you for being responsible for inadvertently stopping Gacy's murdering spree, making the ultimate sacrifice? Would I tell you that the Cubs finally won the World Series? That your parents will never be the same because you died? And Rob, will you ever forgive me for representing the man who killed you?

40.

BIRTHDAY GREETING FROM HELL

Five months after the execution, my life was finally getting back to the pre-Gacy norm. The stress levels had decreased, and I relished being out of the spotlight.

As Greg's 46th birthday was approaching, I began to anticipate the practical joke my late client and I had planned. Late in the evening of October 13, I sneaked downstairs to the kitchen telephone, pulled out my mini-recorder, and left Greg the birthday message he will never forget: the voice of John Wayne Gacy, dead for months, wishing him a happy birthday from the grave.

At 4:45 a.m., I awoke to Greg throwing the covers off the bed. I watched as he leaned over to grab the bedside telephone to check his messages like he did every morning just in case, in his words, "There is a human tragedy that needs my immediate attention."

I watched as he performed his morning routine, retrieving his messages, punching buttons, and triaging the night's dramas and client demands. His whole body froze when he heard what I knew was the voice of his executed client.

I suddenly thought, *Oh my God, what if he has a heart attack from the shock of hearing this message!* Fortunately, that was not at all his reaction. I saw him press more buttons to replay the message. He did it three times and then hung up the phone gently.

He turned to me with a smile. "That was one of the most comforting messages I have ever gotten." Gacy's message was respectful and grateful. If he didn't mean what he said, he sure was convincing in pretending to be.

October 14, 1994, was a glorious fall Friday in Chicago. That evening, I threw my usual elaborate surprise party for Greg—this one over the top. I lured the poor birthday boy to a suburban funeral home (owned by a high school friend) under the pretext that the uncle of a college buddy had died and I had to attend the wake.

When we walked through the door, the sign outside the wake read, "The Internment of Greg Adamski." The room was filled with friends and family dressed in black who eulogized him throughout the evening. A hearse took us to a local restaurant for funeral-themed drinks and dinner. A fitting celebration given the events of the year and the phone message that started the morning.

After the party, Greg turned to me and said he wished Gacy could have been there to see his prank come to fruition. His words from the last day of his life reminded me, "I will never die. Mark my words."

In a way, Gacy was right.

41.

WHO ELSE?

I have doubts about a lot of facts in the case of John Gacy, but I have no doubts that he was responsible for other victims. During his arrest interrogation, he flippantly told one investigator that "45 sounds about right."

He later told another investigator about a body that he had dumped in a nearby forest preserve that he hadn't even bothered to cover. Although he was an exaggerator and a braggart, it rings true that 33 was the tip of his sociopathic iceberg.

The area where Gacy lived is surrounded by acres of forest preserves, walking trails, and a wooded golf course. What would have stopped him from dumping bodies there? It is undisputed that for years he traveled all over the country performing construction jobs for at least two franchises.

His travels took him to areas that were less populated than the Chicago suburbs and some that were decidedly rural. Picking up boys and men in these areas may have been easier as small-town residents are generally more trusting than those in urban areas.

The opportunity to dispose of bodies would be a no-brainer in heavily wooded areas, rivers, and uninhabited properties. At the time, there was no national database for missing persons or unidentified bodies. DNA was in its infancy. When Gacy was questioned about certain missing boys who had connections to him or had worked for him, they strangely failed to see that Gacy had been imprisoned in Iowa for sodomizing an employee, which should have made him a prime candidate for being a repeat sex offender. If he had only one arrest for sexual violence, that would be a coincidence. But a half dozen?

I was very interested in the possibility of other victims. On one call with Gacy, I initiated a discussion about whether he was more prolific than his conviction record showed. Despite his blanket denial about his guilt as to any of the victims, he appeared to be very competitive about his "accomplishments" and wanted to have everyone recognize his superiority. When he talked about these issues, he spoke in the abstract. There were a lot of "what ifs" and "suppose thats." I tried to provoke him.

"JW. You know you're probably not going to be in the *Guinness Book* for long."

"Whataya mean?" He said it like this offended him.

"I mean, there is Henry Lee Lucas in Texas. He's saying that he killed over a hundred and maybe over 200. He's got you beat by at least 67 if my math serves me. He's one bad dude."

Lucas's murders spanned from 1960 to 1983. He was convicted of murdering 11 people and sentenced to death for one. Shortly after his arrest, he started confessing to multiple murders. A task force was created that officially cleared 213 previously unsolved murders as a result of Lucas's confessions.

During this time, Lucas received preferential treatment rarely offered to convicts, with officials frequently taking him out of the prison to restaurants in appreciation for his cooperation. It later turned out that these "confessions" were likely false and that Lucas was a pathological liar.

Strangely, in 1998, Governor George W. Bush commuted Lucas's death sentence to life imprisonment, the only commutation he issued. He had allowed 154 inmates to be executed, one every nine days of his tenure. Why he chose Lucas for his gubernatorial mercy is inexplicable.

In any event, Gacy seemed to know everything about Lucas and was agitated by the possibility that another prolific serial killer could top his record. At the time, there was no internet, and inmates had no access to murder encyclopedias if there were such a thing, but Gacy knew his serial killer facts. He told me that Lucas was a fraud and a "wannabe."

He had made up the confessions, and the prosecutors went along with it so they could close cases without having to do the investigative work. They were all "dumb and stupid," a phrase that Gacy loved and had learned from his father. Conversation closed.

"But John," I argued, "they say there are more victims you killed. Let's just say that you committed these murders. Why wouldn't there have been more?

Gacy hemmed and hawed and tried to divert my attention, and therefore I knew I was getting somewhere. Finally, he said, "Murdering is easy if you know what you're doing. Disposing of bodies is not the hard part. The hard part is finding the people to murder who are not gonna be missed." *Oh*, I thought. *I am listening to the strategy of a human predator.*

Four years after the execution, the possibility of more bodies made big news. A modest apartment building four miles east of the site of Gacy's home on Summerdale became the target of an investigation. In the mid-1970s, his mother, Marion, lived in the basement flat of the five-unit building at Miami and Elston in Chicago. Gacy served as the building maintenance man. Neighbors had seen him digging unexplained trenches in the yard late in the evening and later saw that those trenches were suddenly filled in. Police did not follow up on those leads, and one neighbor reported a police officer saying "... we don't want any more bodies."

In 1998, after retired Chicago homicide detective, William Dorsch—who had seen Gacy digging in the middle of the night firsthand—set off alarm bells following a conversation with a TV producer who asked him about the one case he would re-open if he could. The Better Government Association got involved and the possibility of a dig at the site was leaked to the press.

The Chicago Police Department obtained a warrant.

On the big day, a huge white tent was erected over the

area and no one could see exactly what was going on.

Chicago police used ground-sensitive radar but said there was no sign of human remains. Experts contend the noninvasive, ground-penetrating radar that was used couldn't possibly confirm or deny conclusively the existence of a new Gacy gravesite—digging would need to take place. The case was closed.

In 2013, the site was again "investigated," this time when the ground was firmly frozen in March. Seventeen to 20 targets were identified, but only three were excavated. Authorities announced there were no bodies. However, an expert associated with the case admitted the search was not thorough enough to make any solid conclusions.

Others contend the workers dug in the wrong spots.

To date, there has never been a full excavation of that lot or the driveway, where a teenage assistant to Gacy said he dug a 10 x 10 x 10' hole. It defies logic why this has not been done.

If one family could have closure in identifying a loved one, it would be well worth whatever expense or inconvenience associated with the efforts.

The county officials' reticence to take these actions continues to stoke the theory that there are other victims and that someone is protecting Gacy and perhaps his accomplices.

42.

LIVE OR LET DIE

I didn't write this book to preach against the death penalty. Most people have deep feelings about this issue, and mine are not any more important than anyone else's. However, my book is about how I represented a death row inmate, and as such, it must include the reasons why I fought fiercely against an impending execution for a despised and obviously guilty man.

Over the years, people have challenged my motives for taking on Gacy as a client, and I accept the challenge, but you must believe this: I despise the death penalty. I always have and always will. Some lawyers devote their entire lives to fighting capital punishment. I am not one of them. Gacy was a "one-and-done" death row client. But after having gone through this battle, my beliefs are embedded even more deeply.

From the time I was aware of the issue, I felt a strong visceral reaction to the idea of executions. Why? Perhaps, I have an overabundance of empathy. I could never get on board with the argument that executions are a good thing. Over the years, the concept of confirmation bias likely has ingrained these views. Confirmation bias is the theory that people tend to favor information that confirms their existing beliefs or hypotheses. A person will give more weight to evidence that is consistent with their views and will undervalue evidence that could disprove it. This operates in trials when jurors have deep-seated beliefs about police misconduct, false confessions, racial bias, etc.

Jury experts say if a juror is wired to find a defendant guilty, he will view all evidence through "guilty-as-charged" goggles, and all contrary evidence is ignored or downplayed. This concept has been discussed recently in terms of the polarization of people's opinions which cause them to watch only the news station that confirms their already-entrenched beliefs: Fox if you are conservative and CNN or MSNBC if you are liberal. Consistent with confirmation bias, it is likely I have chosen to spotlight the downsides to the death penalty and diminish and rationalize away the anti-capital punishment arguments. With that warning, here is the way I see it.

Capital punishment is wrong because all human life is valuable. The inalienable right to life cannot be extinguished by the bad acts a person commits. We all do bad things, very few of us on the level of Gacy, but the question is: Who decides at what point our bad acts trump our right to live? I certainly don't want to be the arbiter of life or death. Who am I to judge? If there is a God, perhaps He is the one we should allow to make that determination. It's one thing for a jury to decide someone is guilty and should be incarcerated; it's quite another to ask them to decide if he should cease to live. To subject a group of 12 citizens to sit in judgment of others, deciding whether they live or die, seems like too great a burden on anyone.

Studies have shown that many jurors who have served on a capital murder trial suffer post-traumatic stress and other adverse effects. This could be partly because the facts of a death penalty case are likely to be particularly gruesome to the average person. It may also be due to the burden of having to make such a monumental decision. Jurors who impose a death sentence fare worse after the trial than those who impose a life sentence. Many suffer nightmares, anxiety, and depression for months and sometimes years after their jury service. This, again, supports my contention, which is: It's easy to say, "Kill the bastard." It's much harder to be the one responsible for doing it.

The next argument is that innocent people are regularly executed. Even for people who are against the death penalty, there is always the "Gacy exception," which means even if it's wrong to execute, this man was so clearly guilty, he should be executed.

Nevertheless, if we executed the Gacys of the world, eventually we will execute someone who is less certainly guilty and then down the slippery slope we go until we execute an innocent person.

Studies show that for every nine executions, there is one exoneration—not based upon a technicality, but actual innocence. In each of those wrongful convictions, at least 12 people unanimously found the person guilty beyond any reasonable doubt and also found the person so lacking in worth that he was not fit to live among us. In almost all of these cases, numerous panels of learned judges affirmed those assessments of guilt and condemnation. Wrongful convictions happen—all the time. The worse the crime, the more likely there will be a mistake.

When a crime so offends a community, the police, prosecutors, and the public all want to put an end to the question of who did it. For horrific crimes, we look at the defendant sitting beside his lawyer and assume he wouldn't be sitting there unless he did "something" to deserve it. Better to put him away forever than to risk that he is the one who did the crime; the presumption of innocence be damned.

Even in the case of Gacy, I believe that authorities overlooked evidence that other perpetrators were likely involved in his crimes. There was such a public outcry to close the book on Gacy, it's very possible a simplified case was constructed and a conviction railroaded through.

In 1993, the plight of the innocent was made more onerous when the U.S. Supreme Court ruled that an execution is not unconstitutional even if there is significant evidence of innocence. Yes. That is correct. Our nation's highest court approved of executing an innocent person. As long as he receives his appeals, the fact he did not commit the crime is irrelevant. The justice system in our country is fabulous, but it relies on humans to operate it. As long as humans are fallible, so is the system. Infallibility and the irreversible nature of capital punishment are a deadly combination.

We come to the issue of deterrence. One of the goals of our justice system is to deter others from committing crimes. There is little argument here: Capital punishment does not deter murder, and if it did, it wouldn't deter murder any better than life imprisonment. The vast majority of murderers commit crimes in the heat of passion, by compulsion, fueled by anger, jealousy, drugs and alcohol. They are by definition crimes of impulse. These murderers do not weigh the consequences of their actions in any way. Serial killers' compulsion is so strong that it matters not what possible punishments might result. Knowing that the death penalty looms out there is irrelevant. Serial killer Ted Bundy, an intelligent man who was once a law student, traveled to Florida for his last murderous crime spree, knowing that Florida was a prolific user of the horrific electric chair, "Old Sparky."

The statistics bear out the lack of deterrent effect of the death penalty. The places where the punishment is implemented more frequently do not have lower crime rates, specifically murder rates. A *New York Times* study showed that, over the past 20 years, the homicide rate in states with the death penalty was 48% to 101% higher than states without it. The study also showed that homicide rates rise and fall symmetrically in both death and no-death states, suggesting that the death penalty does not affect criminal conduct.

The death penalty is a harsh punishment, but it is simply not harsh on crime.

Another basic argument is that it defies logic to punish killing by killing. If it is wrong for the defendant to have killed, it is more morally offensive for the state—a reasoned and emotionless body—to take the measured steps to seek vengeance.

As someone who has traveled widely, I believe the fairness we enjoy in the United States is far superior to that which exists almost anywhere in the world. But the use of capital punishment, outlawed in 70% of the world and almost all western societies, puts a huge stain on our nation's canvas. The United States is number six in the world when it comes to the frequency of using capital punishment, behind China, Iran, Saudi Arabia, Iraq, and Egypt. The great Clarence Darrow said in his closing argument in the Leopold and Loeb case, "I would hate to live in a state that I didn't think was better than a murderer."

Many say it is morally mandated that a person who kills should receive equal treatment. They cite the Bible's verse "an eye for an eye, a tooth for a tooth." In essence, there must be quid pro quo retribution. However, biblical scholars will tell you that this is an incorrect interpretation. The "eye for an eye" phrase derives from the Code of Hammurabi, a Babylonian set of legal principles dating back to the 1700s B.C. The Code, one of the most important origins of our law, is depicted in a relief at the U.S. Capitol in Washington, D.C. and the headquarters of the United Nations in New York.

The phrase was meant as a restriction or limit on the amount of compensation that could be given for a loss. It is meant to proscribe a limit on punishment, not mandate equal punishment. The phrase might better be phrased, "only one eye for one eye."

One of the strongest arguments against capital punishment is that it is sought and awarded unevenly, unfairly, and in a discriminatory manner. If we are going to have a punishment that ends a person's most fundamental right, that is, to live, then we should do it in a way that is even-handed, predictable, and without regard for race, gender, income level, jurisdiction, IQ points, or quality of attorney. I am not sure that can ever be achieved as prejudice is an inherent flaw in human nature.

People of color have accounted for a disproportionate 43% of total executions since 1976 and 55% of those currently awaiting execution. The following shows the percentage of minorities on their respective death rows: U.S. Military (86%);

Colorado (80%); U.S. Government (77%); Louisiana (72%); and Pennsylvania (70%).

While white victims account for approximately one-half of all murder victims, 80% of all capital cases involve white victims. As of October 2002, 12 people have been executed where the defendant was white and the murder victim black, compared with 178 black defendants executed for murders with white victims. The odds of getting a death sentence increased three and a half times when the victim is white rather than black. What does that say about the way prosecutors and jurors value life?

Prosecutors have unfettered discretion in deciding which cases become capital cases, seeking the death penalty in approximately one percent of all capital-eligible cases. Among the states that allow the death penalty, approximately 98% of the prosecutors are white.

Let's talk about the cost. Hundreds of people have challenged my opposition to executions by saying that "it costs way too much to keep these people alive. I don't want my taxes going to pay for a bunch of criminals rotting in jail." The evidence is indisputable. It costs more to execute someone than to incarcerate them.

A legislative audit in Kansas found the estimated cost of a death penalty case was 70% more than the cost of a comparable non-death penalty case. Death penalty cases, from inception through execution, cost $1.26 million. Non-death penalty case costs were $740,000. When New Jersey abolished the punishment in 2007, the cost of the state keeping inmates on death row was $72,602 per year for each prisoner, compared to $40,121 per year to keep them in prison, according to a state commission. In Tennessee, death penalty trials cost an average of 48% more than the average cost of trials in which prosecutors seek life imprisonment. In Maryland, death penalty cases cost three times more than non-death penalty cases, or $3 million for a single case. In California, the current system costs $137 million per year; it would cost $11.5 million for a system without the death penalty. In Illinois, a 2010 study documented that over $200 million would have been saved if Illinois had abolished the death penalty in 2000, just ten years before. The price tag of convicting and executing Timothy McVeigh for the Oklahoma City Bombing was over $13 million—and he waived his rights to many available appeals.

Why does the death penalty cost more? Investigative expenses are much higher when death is sought. Death penalty trials have two separate and distinct phases: conviction (guilt/innocence) and sentencing. Jury selection is more complicated, and larger jury pools are required. Both parties generally call experts on issues of DNA, ballistics, mental fitness, etc. Special pretrial and post-trial motions are brought. There are many appeals, retrials, and resentencing trials, and the defendant is entitled to a legal defense along the way.

Death row is more expensive to maintain. When inmates have "nothing to lose," there are higher security concerns due to isolation and observation. The execution itself entails many expenses and other safety concerns, not just for death row, but for general population, as inmates often become agitated and violent when there is an execution.

I will toss you one more argument against executions. Life imprisonment is more punishment than executing someone. Why give the inmate control over ending his appeals and taking the easy way out? Let him rot in his 6x9' cell and mull over the bad choices he made in his life. Let an inmate's monotonous existence in the horrible confines of our states' most deplorable prisons act as an ongoing reminder that murder is wrong.

Now that I have given you my arguments, those of you who abhor capital punishment may have a bit more fodder for your bleeding-heart cannon.

However, those of you who say, "Strap them in the chair!" are likely unmoved by my blather, firm in your view that capital punishment is justified in certain circumstances in general and in Gacy's circumstance in particular. Many of my arguments do not apply to the subject of this book.

43.

WHAT ABOUT THE VICTIMS?

Among the thousands of critical comments I have received about representing Gacy, the most common is: What about the victims? Why do you care more about a murderous, evil pedophile than you do these innocent boys or their families? I understand that sentiment, but as I have explained in prior chapters, my job is to care about and represent the former and not the latter. That doesn't mean I am oblivious to the pain and suffering Gacy caused. How could I be and still be human?

I have not had contact with the victims' families. They have never contacted me. During the writing of this book, I sent a letter to one of the more vocal family members, but not surprisingly, it was returned unopened.

For this reason, I can't very well write about this aspect of the Gacy story. It is not mine to tell, but it seems wrong not to address the fact that Gacy left a trail of destruction and that the victims matter. My guess is that as long as Gacy was alive and making news, his very existence was a raw and piercing arrow into the hearts of those who were affected.

The public is perpetually entertained and fascinated with Gacy due to the media's never-ending rehashing of the story in movies and documentaries, but the victims must suffer greatly when they are aired. I can't imagine how hurtful it is for them to see others being entertained by the very source of their personal tragedies. I realize this book may keep the pain alive. That is one of the reasons I hesitated for 27 years before writing it.

I understand the criticism that the victims are left out of the anti-capital punishment argument, and that is unfair. But as a lawyer involved in the criminal justice system, I have a single-minded focus.

While writing this chapter, I experienced a "what about the victims?" issue as to another high-profile matter. While giving legal analysis on a national news show about the legal basis for comedian Bill Cosby's sudden release from prison on his sexual assault conviction, I told the interviewer that, although I abhor the result, the decision was the correct legal one.

In 2005, Andrea Constand reported that Cosby had drugged her and sexually assaulted her while she was asleep. A deal was cut. The prosecutor would decline prosecution, and in exchange, Cosby would submit to depositions in a civil suit Constand had filed against him. Why did the prosecutor do this? He may have thought the charges would be hard to prove beyond a reasonable doubt due to the "he said/she said" nature of the crime and the fact that Cosby and Constand had been friendly before and after the crime.

Cosby did as agreed. He testified in the depositions and made incriminating statements, which led to him paying Constand $3.38 million to settle the civil suit. Ten years later, a newly elected district attorney took office and decided that Cosby should be prosecuted.

Just before the statute of limitations expired, Cosby was charged with the very crime the prosecutors had agreed not to pursue in 2005. He was convicted and served nearly three years in prison before the Pennsylvania Supreme Court recognized Cosby's argument was correct: When the government promises not to prosecute a crime and a defendant takes actions adverse to his interests based upon that promise, the government's failure to abide by the agreement is a violation of due process. It is particularly egregious because the State used Cosby's own words from the depositions in court to convict him—a violation of his Fifth Amendment right not to incriminate himself. It is clear to me that this was not just a "technicality." It was a violation of basic Constitutional rights.

When I gave that commentary, I said I hated the outcome but approved of the basis for the ruling. Sixty women have come forward to accuse Cosby of doing the same thing to them. I believe these women, and I believe Cosby is a sex offender. Stronger than my belief in Cosby's guilt as a sick and disturbed man who used his celebrity to perpetrate his crimes is my belief in the integrity of our system of justice. The government cannot make a deal and then go back on it. Defendants plead guilty all the time. Ninety-seven percent of all federal cases and 94% of all state cases are plea-bargained. In exchange for a lighter punishment, people admit their guilt. This relieves the criminal justice system of the huge burden of trying these cases, allows the defendant a break, and hopefully helps the victims move on and avoid testifying. The whole system would fall apart if every new prosecutor who came into office could erase all the plea deals and bring the defendants back to court for those crimes. You don't have to be a lawyer to see how grossly unfair that is. Even for a sex offender. Even for a serial sex offender. Even for Bill Cosby.

After my interview was aired, the following post appeared on my Facebook page: "What a surprise from the woman who defended John Wayne Gacy! You have about as much empathy for people/victims as the perpetrators of these horrific crimes. I hope one day you wake up to what you have done and are doing. (Although I doubt VERY MUCH that will happen.)"

This was one of the nicer, G-rated posts, but this is my point: When I say that I am in favor of honoring the Constitution, fairness, and due process, the argument skips to, "You lack empathy and are a bad person." It's easy to make an argument by calling someone a bad person. These comments do not hurt me. They instead lead me to believe that my detractor didn't understand the issue. If he did, he would realize that if the government did that same thing to him, his son, his brother or anyone else, he would be kicking and screaming, "Unfair!"

And who would he turn to as an advocate? Some empathetic, nice lawyer who believes that our Constitution is optional? No. He would hire someone just like me, who would yell and scream until some appellate court heard my argument and ruled on it correctly, honoring the law that makes this country so great.

What no one is saying is this: Why didn't some prosecutor nail Bill Cosby when 60 women suffered at his hands during a span of 56 years in ten states? Were they lazy? Didn't want to rock the boat with a celebrity like Cosby? Afraid to go up against expensive and competent lawyers? Let's talk about empathy. Where was the empathy for the victims on the part of the prosecutors? That is the question that should be answered. And the same can be asked in the Gacy case: Why wasn't he convicted of the several sexual assault cases that occurred over the years? Some of the police reports detail absolute depravity. Why weren't those victims believed?

Lawyers owe their clients undivided loyalty. That does not include thinking about the feelings of the victims. It just doesn't. I am frequently asked to represent victims of crimes—including sex crimes. I have taken on that representation aggressively and wholeheartedly without any regard for the accused, with the specific intent that the perpetrator be sent to jail.

About ten years ago, a 40-year-old man from one of the more affluent northern Chicago suburbs called me to make an appointment. When he arrived at my office, he was red-faced and shaking with anger. A week prior, he had driven his eight-year-old daughter, Pamela, to a pajama party for her best friend. The friend's father, D.S., was an important local politician and wealthy businessman. His house was worth well over $2 million, and everyone in the neighborhood knew him because he performed substantial community work and was politically active.

The ten girls at the party finally went to sleep at about 1 a.m. At about 4 a.m., D.S. crept into the room where Pamela was sleeping. He lifted her nightgown and began to fondle her. When she awoke, he picked her up and carried her to the living room couch where he continued his illicit behavior.

Fortunately, Pamela's parents had taught young Pamela about what was acceptable touching and what was not. She loudly and firmly told D.S. he must stop. She insisted upon calling her parents and would not let up until she was allowed to do so. When her dad picked her up, Pamela immediately gave him a detailed and specific account of what D.S. had done. Her parents called the police, who, after listening to Pamela's accusation with a child advocate present, turned it over to the prosecutor, who declined charges. According to the States Attorney, this situation presented a "he said/she said" scenario, and the testimony of an eight-year-old was unlikely to prove guilt beyond a reasonable doubt.

While the father sat before me trembling with rage, he insisted that D.S. be held accountable for his conduct. At some point, I asked him why he chose me to be his lawyer. He said he wanted a woman because his daughter would feel more comfortable dealing with me. He added that my media and professional connections might allow me to persuade authorities to bring charges. And finally, he wanted a good trial lawyer for his criminal defense because, if the legal system would not make D.S. pay for his actions, he intended to go over to his house with a baseball bat to avenge his daughter.

I proceeded to represent the family and secured the prosecution. When the allegations were made public, several other families reported that D.S. had done inappropriate things with their children. Do I have any empathy for D.S.? Not a chance. Did I do my job by zealously advocating for a crime victim? Yes. Do I care that he went to jail and lost everything? Happy that he did.

Back to the Gacy victims. The one question I would like to ask them is whether Gacy's execution helped their grieving process. I hate the word "closure" as I cannot imagine how there could be closure when you lose a loved one in this way. A brother of one of the victims said after the execution, "I feel like justice has finally been served, but it's been a long time in the making." Others made similar comments.

I have read studies about how victims are affected by capital punishment. Proponents have long argued for the death penalty as necessary to "do justice," but many studies suggest that achieving satisfaction through execution is difficult. There are a growing number of victims who oppose capital punishment and do not want it pursued. There are myriad reasons given. Although most victims do not believe a killer will repent, "there is always a chance for redemption," said Beth Kissileff whose husband was a rabbi killed in the shooting rampage that killed 11 worshippers at a synagogue in Pittsburgh.

The death penalty, for many, provides neither the closure nor healing that the legal and political systems promise. Instead, a growing number of victims' families say it inhibits the healing. One woman whose sister was brutally murdered said that when the murderer was sentenced to death, she was led to believe there would be sudden relief when the execution occurred.

So, she waited for 15 years, eagerly anticipating the execution day.

When it did occur, she felt no relief or closure and realized her years of waiting were a waste of energy. The execution was yet another letdown. The only consolation was that the perpetrator could no longer harm anyone else, a reason that cannot be minimized. In these studies, where the defendant received a life sentence, many victims' families say they felt some sense of relief the process was over and there would be no further legal events in the future.

A Marquette Law School study showed that murder victims' families, where the death penalty was not available, were physically, psychologically, and behaviorally healthier and expressed greater satisfaction with the legal system than families in death penalty cases. Murderers who are sentenced to death are typically followed more closely by the media. Every time there is an appeal in their cases, the story is plastered all over the news.

I have to believe that seeing the face of the person who murdered your loved one on the evening news for over a decade is a constant re-traumatization for the families.

The bottom line is: Who am I to say what gives any comfort to Gacy's victims' families? If the families felt any sense of relief or justice when Gacy was executed, for that I am sincerely glad.

44.

LIFE AFTER DEATH

Have you ever had a time in your life when you look back and realize there was a turning point—a pivotal moment when everything in your life changed? Looking back, I see that the Gacy episode was just that; it altered the current of my life substantially. During the seven months I represented him, much of what was going on was distinctly negative.

The legal losses, the social rejection, and the stress of taking on an impossible task were largely bad things. I lost clients and friends. I donated over $250,000 in legal fees to the cause. But like many things in life, difficulties can lead to positive events. It is hard to say this, but my serial killer client was right. In the long run, my career has been positively affected by being associated with a murderous sociopath.

Less than 30 days after the execution, a former football star named O.J. Simpson took a ride in his white Bronco down a Los Angeles freeway after his ex-wife and her friend were brutally murdered in Brentwood, California. Over 57% of the country's population watched that chase. Simpson was charged with the double murder. The "Trial of the Century," as it was dubbed, grabbed the attention of the public worldwide with 150 million people watching the trial regularly. Local and national media were desperate for legal commentators who could talk about the Simpson case.

My name was on the top of the list, having just buried my

famous client and having spent hundreds of hours giving media interviews. I became an expert in all things O. J. Simpson. To this day, I am asked by national and local television and radio stations to comment on matters ranging from the U.S. Supreme Court decisions to murder cases, to new legislation, employment matters, and celebrity legal stories.

Just after the execution, Greg and I were called by the manager of a well-known local radio station asking us to come in and "do" a two-hour radio show. When we showed up thinking that we were to be interviewed as guests, we were terrified to learn that we were, in fact, the hosts! We talked for two hours without any preparation or experience in hosting a radio show. That launched a 27-year career in hosting radio shows in the Chicago market.

Because of my Gacy experience, I have been the designated legal analyst for the Chicago Fox affiliate for over 25 years, and I have done countless television interviews on national television with the likes Don Lemon, Bill O'Reilly, Megyn Kelly, Larry King, Leeza Gibbons, Maury Povich, Nancy Grace, Montel Williams, and many more. My interviews have been featured in at least 30 Gacy documentaries and in countless news articles.

Just months after Gacy was executed, the dean of my law school, University of Illinois College of Law, a respected tier-one law school at the time, came to Chicago to meet with me. I thought it was about donating to the alumni fund, something I was not in a position to do, given a drastic drop in income due to a certain deceased client. To my amazement, he told me he wanted to appoint me as an adjunct professor of law to teach a course on—you guessed it—The Death Penalty. Faculty positions at most law schools are reserved for academic-type lawyers. I certainly was not one. If my GPA in law school were a baseball pitcher's earned run average, I would have been a Cy Young winner. Nothing against my intellect, but I was too busy working full-time putting myself through school to devote the proper time to my studies.

I was stunned by this request. I later told the dean my

teaching the death penalty was like the captain of the Exxon Valdez teaching a class on boating safety. Despite losing my one and only capital punishment case, I became an expert on death penalty jurisprudence and ended up teaching courses at Illinois and other law schools for 20 years.

How did handling this case affect my law practice? This is the strangest part. Because I represented a prolific killer, losing almost all legal challenges along the way, clients and others seem to have more respect for me as a lawyer. Does it make sense? I don't think so, but I can explain it.

I assume that people think if the likes of John Gacy chose me to try to save his life in the most difficult of situations, I must be a good lawyer. Only good lawyers get chosen for the tough cases. Think, Clarence Darrow, Alan Dershowitz, F. Lee Bailey. It would be ridiculous to put myself in the same league as these lawyers, but the same analysis applies. Even Marcia Clark was given a television show after losing a case that many thought was a slam dunk conviction, given DNA and motive evidence directly tying O.J. Simpson to the crime. The lawyers involved with Gacy did pretty well themselves. Gacy's first defense lawyer, Sam Amirante, and prosecutor Bill Kunkle, both became judges and then successful practitioners. Likewise for prosecutor Terry Sullivan, who has been a well-known legal analyst for decades on a prominent Chicago news station.

With Gacy dead, my representation of him became more palatable to others. With no madman alive, my stories about him were welcomed at cocktail parties and at colleges, bar associations, community groups, professional women's groups, and seminars where I was asked to speak about my experience. I am an oddity. I have done something very few have done. And at least I have lived to tell about it.

One year after the execution, I was in San Diego taking the California bar exam and stumbled upon the Death Museum. Curious, I walked inside. Immediately the "curator" recognized me, ushered me in to show me the collection of killers' artwork, and asked for my autograph. Before I left, he had given me a lifetime membership.

There hasn't been a week that has passed in the last 27

years when I have not received mail, email, phone calls, or some communication about representing Gacy. Some are from collectors wanting to buy memorabilia. Others are high school students writing papers on serial killers. Many are weirdos asking me about or accusing me of strange sexual practices with or without Gacy, while others are angry and threatening.

At least ten men have contacted me to attempt to confirm their recollection that they met or had been picked up by Gacy and had narrowly escaped being victims. I have been asked to participate in a John Gacy séance, to be the judge in a Halloween horror costume competition, and to host a serial killer jeopardy game for charity. Handling this case has made me a legal novelty whether I like it or not.

Comments remain the same to this day. People who hear that I represented Gacy say, instinctively, "How could you? Why would you?" And without really listening to the answer or caring what I say, they then ask the real question they want answered: "What was he like? What was it like to know John Wayne Gacy?"

Now that you have read my book, you know.

45.

EPILOGUE

On February 14, 2011, my dear husband, Greg Adamski, died.

Greg was an early riser and was usually up by 4:30 a.m. to begin his workday, so when I awoke at 6:30 a.m. to see him still in bed beside me, I immediately knew he had passed. Apparently, he had a heart attack in his sleep. How ironic that this big-hearted man's heart gave out on Valentine's Day.

When the paramedics left my home with Greg's body, I found a card and gifts on his desk. He would have given them to me along with the cup of coffee he brought me in bed every morning for 20 years. His death devastated me. He was my best friend, my lover, my business partner, and my partner in fun.

Most of you reading this have experienced the loss of a loved one. We all grieve differently, and we all carry the scars of that loss. Wrong or right, the way I handled it was to push ahead. I got up the next day and forced myself to go to the office. I followed my regime of exercise and socializing, and forced myself not to spend time wallowing in my misery. Although people were a little disturbed that I was not outwardly showing my despair, I was shattered inside.

I made a habit of allowing myself 30 minutes a day to sit on my bed and cry my eyes out; 60 minutes on weekends. After my sob session was over, I would get up, fix my makeup and continue my day. I took down all photographs of Greg and put them in a large box. When I felt able to look at them, I did, and then put them away again.

I fought very hard to control the dark veil of sadness that wanted desperately to overwhelm my being. I also had a routine that will strike you as strange. I still do it from time to time. While I am at my law office, I close the door and sit down in one of the client chairs facing my desk and the empty leather executive chair in which I imagine Greg sitting. I talk to him. I ask him what I should be doing and thinking. I tell him how I am and relate something funny that happened to me during the day. Then, I close my eyes and listen.

After 21 years at his side, I can hear Greg's voice and laughter. He almost always says the same thing: "You're doing great. Just keep doing what you are doing. I am proud of you." And most of the time, that is all I need.

About one year after my husband's death, while still shaken from this tragic loss, I was set up on a blind date, something I had never done in my 49 years. I was so disinterested that I did not bother to Google the candidate.

"Jerry" called me the next day. He was very pleasant and suggested we meet for dinner the following week. I agreed. Every day, I picked up the phone to cancel, but I just never got around to doing it. Jerry sounded so nice and kind that I didn't have the heart to do it. Besides, what else did I have to do on Saturday night other than cry my eyes out?

When the evening arrived, I was all nerves. I was so out of the dating scene. Jerry was very tall and handsome, but he had a sadness in his eyes. We sat down to dinner at a bustling Italian restaurant, and after our salads arrived, I asked him about his divorce. Divorce? My wife died. I had no idea. It turns out she died three days before Greg from a four-year bout with ovarian cancer. He asked me how long I had been divorced. When I told him that Greg died suddenly of a heart attack three days after his wife died, he was shocked. Neither of us knew going into the date that we had widowhood in common.

One date led to another. Jerry's grief over the loss of his wife helped me leave my personal pity party and look outside myself. With the focus on my sadness redirected, I found that helping someone else overcome theirs was cathartic and energizing. It gave me a purpose.

When you lose a loved one, you think that being loved is what you miss. But you also miss undertaking the love and care of another person; having that purposeful devotion to another human being; putting their interests before your own and contributing to their happiness.

Jerry and I married in 2015. My husband is the complete opposite of Greg. He is quiet, cautious, and in favor of capital punishment, a topic we avoid.

This second chance at love teaches me that what you love about a person is not what they look like, what they do for a living, or if they like the Cubs or the Sox. What you love is the essence of a person. Loyalty. A zest for life. The ability to give. A desire to laugh.

As my friend, the great Judge William Bauer, said while performing our marriage ceremony, "I don't care how important you are, how rich you are or how smart you are. If you don't have one person in your life who has your back, you have absolutely nothing." Interestingly, Jerry's last name, Ricordati, is the command form of the Italian word: "Remember!" Although I will never forget Greg, Jerry helped me remember to live and love again.

People often ask me if I ever handled another death penalty case. Although I was asked to do so several times, I declined. I felt that I had made my contribution to the cause and was not willing to carry the emotional weight of another condemned inmate.

Greg's son, Rik, got his master's degree and has a great job as an urban planner in Texas.

My father, the man whose words made thousands laugh for five decades, suffered a stroke, which, in a cruel and ironic twist of fate, left him without the ability to speak. Despite this major setback, he lived another five years in good humor. Although he couldn't talk, he was still able to communicate, often telling jokes on a little pad of paper he kept in his pocket at all times. His favorite: "My daughter is a criminal lawyer.

Sounds redundant, doesn't it?"

Gacy's sister, Karen Kuzma, is living in another state with her husband of many years. She is a cancer survivor and is close to her children and grandchildren. Although her brother's actions and execution weigh heavily on her, over time, that pain has eased. She has been active in helping families of prisoners deal with their losses. She has written about this topic in her book, *Silent Victims*. She's a woman of faith, which has guided her through these difficulties.

I don't know where Gacy's children are. They have changed their names, and my guess is that no one who knows them has any idea who their father was. His nephew, A.R., moved out west. We are friends on Facebook, and he seems to find peace in being away from the city and taking part in outdoor activities. A.R. loved his uncle and he, too, was devastated by the revelation of the crimes and his execution. Many years after the execution, I said to A.R., "If your uncle had been born 20 years later and had access to all of the homosexual content online, do you think he would not have felt the need to commit these crimes?"

A.R. turned to me solemnly and said, "John online? Karen, if John had the ability to troll for victims on the internet, there would have been 200 more of them."

That was chilling.

Bill Kunkle, Gacy's prosecutor, was a friend of mine. When I taught the death penalty at the University of Illinois on Saturday mornings, he generously volunteered to drive the 135 miles to give my class the best argument in favor of the death penalty. He was an excellent lawyer and believed to the core that the death penalty is the only just sentence for the worst in our society. Bill enjoyed a long, successful career as a big firm lawyer, and then a judge. In retirement, he golfed and sent interesting emails in his free time, before passing in 2022.

Sam Amirante, Gacy's trial lawyer, has also had an excellent career. He served as a well-respected and compassionate judge for over 16 years. He is now in private practice, handling, among other cases, criminal matters. However, I assume all of them are fairly mundane in comparison with the first one of his career. I see him from time to time in court and in Italian restaurants throughout Chicago. As he was Gacy's first lawyer and I was his last, I feel a strange bond with him and always will.

Antoine was released from prison early, sometime in 2019. He contacted me several months ago seeking my help in finding him a place to live. He seemed sober and healthy and told me he had a very nice girlfriend and a pet cat named Snow. He was receiving disability benefits due to his injuries from the armed robbery and a diagnosis of major depression. I helped him find public housing, and we promised to get together in person when we could. He told me he tries to read a paper whenever he can. His favorite section is sports, especially basketball stories. His daughter is grown, and he has several grandchildren. My hope is that he stays clean and on the right side of the law.

Gacy, or his cremains, are buried at an undisclosed location, which the family does not discuss. However, his brain is elsewhere. After the execution, it was removed from his body and examined by a local psychiatrist. She found absolutely nothing abnormal about the organ. She had spent over 50 hours talking to Gacy before his trial and testified that he was insane at the time of his crimes and had no ability to control his conduct. He would have committed the murders, she said, even if a uniformed police officer had been standing nearby looking on.

Up until several months ago, the psychiatrist still had Gacy's brain in her Chicago home, fittingly in the basement, when his sister Karen called me to ask a favor. She had heard that the good doctor was preparing to sell the brain to a reality show ghost hunter for $1 million.

Karen wanted possession of the brain so this could not happen. She was outraged by the thought of her brother's body part being used in this way. She asked me to contact the doctor. After several stern demand letters questioning her right to possess it, the brain was delivered to my law office in a box marked, *DO NOT TILT OR TURN OVER.*

When I saw it, I thought, *At last some legal effort for the Gacy family was successful.*

I can almost hear Gacy himself quipping, "Mess around with Dollface? You have to have your head examined."

I still have the three paintings Gacy gifted to me. The canvases are a bit warped from being stored in my basement for so many years. Once in a while, I go online to see how much people are paying for these horrific pieces of art. I just can't bring myself to make money from selling them. I also cannot bear to display them anywhere. They sit face down on the floor of a closet.

I also have some cards and notes that Gacy gave me, stored away in a file in my basement. I check Ebay occasionally to see if there is any Gacy memorabilia for sale. In particular, I wonder if I will see *The Body Book*, Gacy's macabre catalog of victims, perhaps taken from his cell by a souvenir-seeking prison guard.

Several pieces of crime scene evidence are still stored in Cicero, Illinois, at the Cook County Clerk of Court Records and Storage Imaging Center. Among them are a ligature and set of handcuffs Gacy used to strangle his victims; a police spotlight Gacy put on his car to impersonate a police officer when trolling for men; the blue ski jacket worn by his last victim, Robert Piest; the handwritten map Gacy made for the police showing where the bodies were buried; and the wooden frame door that led to the crawlspace where the remains were found.

Many items that were removed from Gacy's home following his arrest, including several clown suits and other clown memorabilia, have never been recovered.

Seventeen years after Gacy's execution, less than a month after Greg died, the Illinois governor signed a bill abolishing the death penalty. At a somber, sparsely attended event, Governor Pat Quinn signed a bill ending capital punishment in the state.

In the 15 years preceding this event, 21 men in Illinois had been released from death row based upon actual innocence, some mere hours away from lethal injection. At the time, 15 states had abolished the death penalty, and after Illinois, other states followed suit including Virginia, a traditionally active capital punishment state.

Four other states—Oregon, Pennsylvania, Ohio, and California—currently have formal or de facto moratoriums on executions, meaning that more than half the states have now abandoned the practice. It's unlikely that there will be any federal executions as long as President Joe Biden is in office given his campaign pledge to "work to pass legislation to eliminate the death penalty at the federal level." He is the first U.S. president to be openly in favor of abolishing executions.

Public opinion about capital punishment, which has waxed and waned over the years, has made a dramatic nosedive. As of 2019, a Gallup Poll found that a 60% majority of Americans favor life without parole over death as a punishment for murder. That was up from 46% in 2010.

I also think our "woke" culture of young people does not have the heart for executions.

Just a few years ago, I was teaching a law school course at DePaul University. It was the first day of class in the fall semester, and I asked my 20 students to introduce themselves and talk about their professional goals.

Finally, when it was my turn, I told the class about my career and mentioned that I had represented John Wayne Gacy in the last set of his death row appeals. The experience was unusual and career-defining, and because several of the students were interested in criminal law, I thought they might want to ask me questions about it.

After I made my disclosure, the class went silent. The students looked blankly at each other, and one finally raised his hand. "Professor Conti, who is John Wayne Gacy?"

I was stunned.

"Are you telling me that none of you knows who he was?"

The students nodded, even the ones who had been born and raised in the Chicago area. I proceeded to explain who he was, something I had never, ever had to do.

I finally said, "I can't believe you don't know who Gacy was."

The same student who had raised his hand before said

in typical young people upspeak, "Like, Professor Conti, we weren't even alive in 1979, and our parents were, like, five years old?"

Hmm, I thought. *I wasn't alive in 1888, but I know who Jack the Ripper was.*

I cannot attribute the students' lack of knowledge to a lack of access to information. In my youth, if I wanted information I had to walk to the library, use the card catalog, and retrieve a book from the shelves. Now we have Google—and Alexa/Siri if your hands are occupied. I can only surmise that either the students did not have the curiosity to learn about historical events that did not affect them, or perhaps the Gacy story was so far in the past that it was fading from view. Frankly, the latter is hard for me to believe. Given the number of docuseries and books coming out every year, I think the Gacy story, as he himself told me, will never go away.

I accept that am still associated with John Wayne Gacy and will always be. I would rather the association be with my fight against the death penalty, but you don't get to choose your legacy. I respect the public's hatred of the Gacys of the world. It is only right to hate evil, destruction, the taking of human life, and all things inhumane.

All I ask is that when people view my actions, they understand I was simply following my moral roadmap and zealously advocating for my client as I have been sworn to do.

Shakespeare said, "The evil that men do lives after them."

While Gacy's evil is sure to live on, I hope that for myself and others out there who take on unpopular causes, people will also remember our efforts to do what we believe is just.

PHOTO GALLERY

Photos Courtesy of Karen Conti with Permission from Karen Kuzma.
Top: The Gacy siblings. John Wayne Gacy was six. Bottom: Gacy at approximately 18 years old with his mother and sister, Karen.

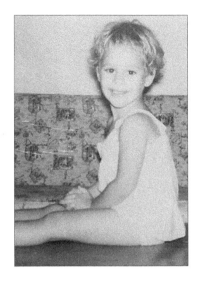

Photos Courtesy of Karen Conti.

Left: Karen, age 3 or 4. Right: Karen's mother, Marilyn Conti, during her days as a member of a national dance troupe.

Photos Courtesy of Karen Conti.

Left: Joe Conti, Karen's father, was always quick to joke. Right: Attorney Greg Adamski, Karen's legal and life partner.

Photo Courtesy of Karen Conti.

Karen's childhood home (photographed above) looks nearly identical to the John Wayne Gacy childhood home released in other photographs by the media.

Public Domain Photographs.

Left: Gacy as a young boy. This photo was released to the public by the Clark County Indiana Prosecutor's Office. Right: Gacy with former First Lady Rosalynn Carter in a photograph taken by a White House photographer.

Division of Supervision of Parolees	Form 20 Chicago
Parole Face Sheet — Leaflet	
Illinois State Penitentiary	IOWA Branch

Name GACY, John	No. ANA-26526
Alias	
Received 12-11-68	County Blackhawk
Crime Sodomy	Plea
Date of Sentence 12-3-68	Sentence 10 years
Judge Van Metre	Attorney
Color White	Nativity Ill.
Citizen Age 28	Height 5-8 Weight 205
Occupation Cook	Prison Conduct
Married Div.	Wife Living
Children 2	Living
Correspondent	
Previous Criminal Record See File	
Action Acc. for supervision-6-19-70	
First Parole Date 6-18-70	Second Parole
Emp. Bruno's Restaurant	
Add. 126 N. Wells St.	

Public Record Document.

Gacy's 1968 Parole Fact Sheet from the Division of Supervision of Parolees, Illinois State Penitentiary. Signs pointing to the monster hidden inside Gacy appeared early on.

Public Domain Photographs.

Law enforcement released a number of photos, including the now-infamous picture of Gacy dressed in his clown costume. The top left booking photo is from his early sodomy conviction prior to the murders. Several later mugshots were taken by the Illinois Department of Corrections, the Des Plaines, Illinois Police Department and other public agencies.

Photos Courtesy of Bill Kunkel.

Above: Karen was given these photos by Gacy prosecutor Bill Kunkel. They show the inside of the courtroom in which Gacy was tried. The lower photo shows the crawlspace entrance to Gacy's home, which was removed from the house and brought to the court as evidence.

Photo Courtesy of Karen Conti.

On the steps of the U.S. Supreme Court with opposing counsel after the 1990 argument.

Photos Courtesy of Karen Conti.
Karen and Greg with John Wayne Gacy on death row around November 1993.

KILLING TIME WITH JOHN WAYNE GACY 263

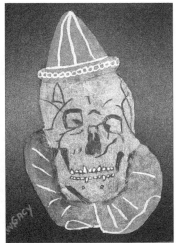

Photos Courtesy of Karen Conti.

Gacy painted this version of his Pogo the Clown portrait for Karen while on death row. His clown skull paintings are among some of his most popular with collectors, and he gifted the one at the top right to Karen. Finally, Gacy painted and gave this seascape to her right before his execution. She would store them away, never displaying them.

Photos Courtesy of Karen Conti.

Greg and Karen outside the penitentiary during one of their many trips there to visit with their client.

KILLING TIME WITH JOHN WAYNE GACY 265

Public Record Document.

John Wayne Gacy's death certificate filed in the State of Illinois.

Photos Courtesy of Karen Conti.
Top: Karen with attorney Marcia Clark of O.J. Simpson trial fame.
Bottom: Supreme Court Justice Sandra Day O'Connor.

Photos Courtesy of Karen Conti.
Top: Greg and Karen appear on one of their first radio shows.
Bottom: Greg and Karen ten years after Gacy's execution.

Photos Courtesy of Karen Conti.

Top: Karen walks the media bank giving legal commentary during the Drew Peterson murder trial. Bottom: Karen as host of her own radio show in Chicago.

Photos Courtesy of Karen Conti.

Top: Karen with Gacy's sister, Karen, who was profoundly affected by both her brother's actions and execution. Bottom: With husband, Jerry.

Photos Courtesy of Karen Conti.
John Wayne Gacy's brain was delivered by surprise to Karen, who had just begun representing his sister in efforts to halt its sale for $1 million to a reality TV ghost hunter.